RUNNING A HAPPY FAMILY

Running a Happy Family

HOW YOU CAN APPLY WHAT BUSINESS
HAS DISCOVERED ABOUT MANAGEMENT AND
HUMAN RELATIONS TO MAKE AN EFFICIENT
HOME AND A HAPPY FAMILY

Henry and Elizabeth Swift

ILLUSTRATED

THE JOHN DAY COMPANY
NEW YORK

Contents

Foreword

The chief purpose of this book is to point out to parents that certain human-relations skills and techniques currently being taught and used in the business world may also be helpful at home. Application of these skills has lagged behind in the home, despite the fact that they are based on common sense and on sound theory.

The widespread attention being given by business and industry to management training and development led us to the writing of *Running a Happy Family*. In the business world, millions of dollars are being spent to teach everyone from foreman to president how to be a more effective manager or supervisor. Some concerns have worked out extensive programs of their own; others send their men to colleges or professional schools, or call in management-consulting firms. These activ-

ities form the most significant development in the field
of adult education in many years.

Parents of young children well know the total dis-
integration which can occur from time to time in the
average household, no matter how devoted to one another its members may ordinarily be. We believe that
the methods of dealing with people which are now being used in business can be taken home at five o'clock to
benefit those people about whom we care most—our
own families.

Some parents may object that they do not have time
to learn new skills or to read about methods which seem
so obvious. And yet most of them do manage to find
time for nagging, scolding, and cajoling their children.
By using a more constructive approach, they could in
the same time or less produce superior results, and
could teach their children ways of getting along with
others which would benefit them throughout their lives.

This book is not a psychology text, nor is it a treatise
by experts in human relations. It is not an attempt to
show all the right ways—or The Only Right Way—of
influencing human behavior. We know that you cannot
run a home like an office. Much of the highly trained
efficiency and technical methods of the business world
are neither practical nor desirable in the home. But just
as the typewriter or office stapler can sometimes come in
handy for a domestic project, so can some of the simple
pointers from books, articles, and courses that are aimed
at the business world. We do not propose these skills
as a substitute for Tender Loving Care. On the con-

trary, we are convinced that a warmer, closer family life can result from using these ways of eliminating familiar sources of misunderstanding and irritation on the part of both parents and children.

The ideas presented in this book do not work for us all the time. Sometimes we forget to apply them, and sometimes we are in no mood to do so. But we have found that an awareness of good and bad ways to deal with our children and an increased interest in analyzing what has gone wrong have been of tremendous value to all the family. Without offering the book as a panacea, we hope that at least an occasional difficult home situation may be resolved as a result of reading these pages.

H. S.
E. S.

RUNNING A HAPPY FAMILY

I

Talking, Listening, and Understanding

FRANK AND MARY STEVENS are eagerly waiting for the school bus to arrive with their children, Philip and Kate. It is a beautiful afternoon in early June, and they are cheerful and smiling with anticipation. Let us watch its arrival and see what a mess these nice well-meaning people can get into with their children.

For over a week Frank and Mary have been planning a big surprise for Philip and Kate. With the orchards in shape after a lot of hard work, it now looks as though Frank can get away for a couple of days for the first time since early spring.

Enter Philip and Kate.

"Hi, kids! How was school?"

"Good."

"Fine."

"How would you like to pack up your things right now and head up to the lake for an overnight camping trip?" The children's eyes open wide, but neither one speaks.

"Well, how about it? Won't it be fun to go camping?"

Philip is obviously torn. "Gee, yes, but. . . ." (The classic youthful response. Beware when you hear this one, Father!)

"But what?"

"But our class picnic is tomorrow. I told you ages ago."

Kate chimes in, not even doubtful: "And I'm going to Cindy's for lunch and the movies."

Philip is ten, and the class picnic is Very Important. At eight, Kate does not get to see many movies, and her favorite television star is playing.

"But we'll have a whole weekend of picnics! And wouldn't you rather go camping than go to an old movie?" (Possibly, Mother, but how do you like to change your plans in sixty seconds? Not many children are as flexible as all that.)

"This is a wonderful chance for us all to really enjoy the woods. We've borrowed the Blacks' tent and sleeping bags. I've arranged with Uncle Peter to keep track of things here, and Mother has been knocking herself out all week to get everything ready. You ought to be pretty pleased at a chance like this. It may be the only time we can go all year."

This is not the best possible start for a weekend of

camping pleasure. Our fond parents have assumed that the children would want to go camping, and have gone ahead without consulting them or checking on their plans. *And why not?* they assume. *We know what they'll enjoy.*

A little more arguing ensues, but Frank and Mary are too persuasive for the children to hold out much longer. The movie and the class picnic are by-passed (but not forgotten) and the Stevens family heads for the woods. Let us listen in again as they arrive at the chosen campsite.

Frank makes the opening pronouncement: "Okay now, Phil. You get out the tent and I'll show you what to do."

"Oh, I know how to do it. I put one up at Pete's last year."

"Well, be sure the stakes are firm. . . ." Frank shouts a stream of instructions over his shoulder as he turns to help Mary with the cooking equipment. Philip hears none of them, his mind and ears closed as he struggles with the ropes and tries to remember how it went last time at Pete's. He is so sure that he knows how to do it that there is no need to listen to his father.

Frank is busy with the next project. "Here, Kate, you can help me with the fire. First get a little piece of paper, and I'll get the wood."

Kate darts off, and returns with a scrap of newspaper, about three inches square. "Here's the paper, Dad. Can I help light it?"

"Do you think I can light a fire with *that* little piece?"

"But you *said* a little piece." (Talk your way out of that one, Father.)

Frank finds more paper, grumbling at her lack of understanding as he tries to instruct Kate in fire building. *How do you get kids to know what you mean, anyway? They never seem to get it.*

Twenty minutes later Frank returns to check on Philip and the tent. Philip is not in sight; the tent is still a tangle of ropes, stakes, and crumpled canvas. "What's the matter here? Where's Philip?"

Philip is sitting behind a tree, whittling a stick for cooking hot dogs. "Here I am. You want me, Dad?"

"I sure do. Come here. Look at this tent! I thought you were setting it up. What about it?"

"There's something the matter with it."

"I'll say there is. It's in a worse mess than when you started. Why didn't you tell me you didn't know how to do it?" (That's easy. He was afraid to.)

"But I do know how! I did it at Pete's. This old tent . . . There must be something the matter with it."

"Nonsense! There's nothing the matter with the tent. There's something the matter with you, if you ask me. Saying you could do it . . ." Frank scolds on. By now he is hot and tired himself, and takes out his exasperation on Philip, finally ordering him off to sit on a nearby rock while he puts up the tent himself.

Mary comes along, unaware of the argument between Philip and his father. "Why don't you go for a swim,

Phil? It's hot." Philip has been smarting from what he considers an unjustified scolding. He takes off for the lake at the run. When Frank catches sight of him, he explodes like a warm bottle of soda.

"Where's Philip going? I told him to stay right here!"

"But I told him he could go for a swim, Frank. It's hot."

"I know it's hot. I'm hot too. But he's being punished!"

"Well, why didn't you tell me?"

Let's cut the camping scene right here, and see whether Frank has as much trouble getting his ideas across to other people as he has to his own family. The camping trip is an interlude in Frank's busy life as a fruit grower. He is considered to be one of the county's most up-and-coming young farmers, because he has studied both the business side and the scientific side of farming. Frank knows how important the human factor is in running an orchard, just as it is in any business enterprise.

Not long ago, for example, Frank and his brother Peter had to set up the schedule for spraying the fruit trees. The two brothers run the orchards together, along with three regular helpers and a number of extra workers who come in at busy times. In working out the timing for the spring spraying, Frank and Peter looked over the calendar together, and called in their helpers. They consulted with all of them to see whether starting the spraying the following week would conflict with other chores or personal plans. Talking it over, they agreed that by starting on the following Monday, with subsequent sprayings to follow at regular intervals, the whole job would be done by Memorial Day. When everyone's questions were answered, the calendar was marked and posted on the door where it could be easily seen by all the workers. Frank would never commit himself, his brother, and their men to a full season's schedule without discussing it with all of them. He knows better than that.

He also knows how to set up the spraying project in detail for the men who are working for him. If a newly hired worker says "Oh sure, I know what you mean!" would Frank leave it at that? Not Frank. He knows better than *that,* too. The new man might use weed killer instead of insecticide. Frank goes over every step with his men; makes them review the proportions after he has given them; makes absolutely sure they are thinking in the same terms. Furthermore, he would never use such a loose term as "a little spray" or "a few trees." He has learned to specify exact quantities to the men who work in the orchards. He has even learned to overcome the language barriers that are encountered with some of the itinerant workers. Several of them speak almost no English, but Frank makes every effort to make sure that they understand what is expected of them. He knows how important that can be—in the orchard.

Whatever the problem or the project in the orchards, Frank tries hard to keep information flowing back and forth in both directions. He and Peter keep their men informed of plans at each step along the way. They also welcome suggestions, questions, and comments from the men. They know they could not run a successful fruit business if the men were afraid to tell them of broken equipment, quotas not filled, or deadlines not met. They greet all reports, bad or good, with understanding and constructive comments. It all seems so logical as part of running a business enterprise, whether the product is apples or machine tools.

Logical or no, it does not seem to occur to Frank that the same principles might also work well on the home scene. For that matter, now and then nothing quite works out on the home scene. Let us return to the campers for one more look. A swim and supper helped solve most of their difficulties, but there is one last hurdle before the moon rises and peace descends. Who is going to sleep where? Philip wants his sleeping bag under the big pine tree. Kate has been counting on scooping out a snug spot on the beach. Mary and Frank think everyone should be near together, within hearing distance. Everyone is tired. Who will make the decision? Frankly, we give up. We know of no technique guaranteed to solve amicably a dispute between tired children at bedtime. It is one of the insurmountable barriers to communication—fully eight feet high. Our only suggestion is to flip a coin and hope for the best. They will have to quiet down eventually out of sheer fatigue.

DO'S AND DON'TS OF COMMUNICATION

DO'S:

1. *Keep Everyone Informed.* In planning a family venture, consult everyone who is involved—ahead of time and at every step along the way. By neglecting to include Philip and Kate in the plans for their camping trip, their parents ran the risk of spoiling their pleasure in the whole weekend. On his job, Frank was careful to consult with all the other men and to be sure all understood the spraying plans.

2. *Encourage Suggestions, Questions, and Observations.* Keeping the door open for all comments, however unimportant they may seem, will improve morale and keep everyone alert. Frank knows that he could not run an efficient farming enterprise without such contributions from all the workers. But sometimes he forgets that his children can contribute bright ideas which will help the whole family, even though they are "just kids."

3. *Make Sure You Have the Other Person's Full Attention.* If he is too absorbed in something else, make an effort to break through or wait for a more opportune moment. Philip's mind was closed to his father's suggestions while he struggled with the tent. Frank would recognize this situation if a farm worker were trying to start a balky tractor. He should try to do the same with Philip.

4. *Make Good Use of Appropriate Aids to Communication.* Calendars, telephone message pads, bulletin boards, can be of great help in an attempt to keep the

family informed. The spraying schedule was posted in an obvious spot for all to see. Too bad the date of Philip's class picnic was not given equal prominence—he would have appreciated it.

DON'TS:

1. *Don't Let a Mechanical Language Barrier Block Communication.* Whether the difficulty lies in interpretation or knowledge of the language, it is important to recognize this barrier and make a particular effort to overcome it. Frank works hard to make sure that his itinerant workers understand directions. He should do the same at home, and not lose his temper when "a little piece" means something quite different to Kate from what it means to him.

2. *Don't Treat Everyone the Same When Passing on Information.* Differences in age and experience provide different requirements as to what each person needs to be told. On the farm, Frank knows that his migrant workers need more instruction than his regular helpers. He would do well to remember this when giving instructions to his children on how to set up camp.

3. *Don't Let Fear of Reprisal Interfere with Communication.* Try to have an understanding and constructive approach to reports on mistakes, losses, or damage. Philip retreated rather than tell his father that he was unable to manage the tent after all. If Frank's apple pickers are not afraid to tell him when something has gone wrong, surely his children should not feel any such fear of their father's criticism.

4. *Don't Try to Solve Serious Problems When All Are Overtired.* Timing can be all-important. Fatigue and the emotions it produces constitute one of the most substantial barriers to communication and understanding. Frank was too hot and tired to see Philip's disobedience in its proper perspective. He would not discipline a farm worker at the end of a long hard day of spraying, although this is a difficult rule to remember at home or at work. In fact, solving the sleeping arrangement problem amicably was all but an impossibility!

* * *

Communication represents the primary tool for exchanging ideas, and for effecting behavior changes and development. The fundamental problem of dealing with people in business, at home, and in the community is one of mutual understanding. The term *communication* has been used too loosely and too frequently—to the point of becoming a fad. But the importance of getting ideas across to family, friends, neighbors, tradesmen, and business associates cannot be overestimated. Proper communication includes more than the techniques of speaking clearly, posting notices, and keeping people informed through similar mechanical aids. It represents a complex network of meaning, a continuous process of telling, listening, and understanding.

In this chapter we are discussing the importance of communication to the family, with emphasis on the barriers which may be involved, and how to avoid or overcome them. We believe that with the exception of problems of health, most of the difficulties arising in the home are due to faulty communication. These may include a general lack of understanding; failure to keep one another informed; misinterpretation of each person's role in the family; the inability to listen; or failure to appreciate individual differences.

Problems of understanding continually arise within the family. We may think it unnecessary to spell out simple precepts, and assume that we are showing our children how to behave by our own good example. But are they always able to understand our intentions? We enjoy watching the two-year-old mimic our every move and word, but recognize that at his age he cannot understand what he is doing. For different reasons, the same may apply to older children, right up to voting age—or beyond.

Life can be made pleasanter for a great many families if parents will recognize problems of communication and keep them in mind when they try to analyze why things go wrong at home, and why their children behave as they do. Even if they cannot solve all their problems in this manner, life will seem more bearable if they can learn to recognize what causes them. Most people are willing to spend considerable time and money to obtain an answer from a doctor rather than have an unknown illness gnaw away at them. But they overlook the fact that minor irritations of day-to-day family relations which are allowed to go undiagnosed and unattended can also interfere with normal enjoyment of family life.

Even with proper communication in the home, there

is bound to be some strife within the family group. The twins will still fight; and Mother will have to raise her voice occasionally. But the more the family members talk to one another; the more they confide in each other; the more they know and understand about the other members and their various points of view—the happier all will be.

With frequent indications of interest from their parents, children grow more willing to talk over their problems of school or play. We do not mean that every innermost thought or teen-age secret should be blurted out at the supper table for all ears to hear, but just that too many unexpressed thoughts—hopes or fears, likes or dislikes—can lead to a grim and silent atmosphere.

Close relations among all members of the family result in well adjusted children who feel secure in the family group. If you will look around at the families you regard as happy and relaxed, the chances are that you will find they are families that make a real effort toward proper communication in their homes.

Fewer misunderstandings occur when the lines of communication are always open. If children are aware of family objectives and know the reasons behind the things they are asked to do, they will be able to improve their performance of daily chores and come closer to their long-range goals, such as satisfactory school grades.

There are numerous obstacles in the road to good communication. Individual differences of age, personality, and experience, for example, create barriers which require careful consideration. The atmosphere in the

home, or, as the businessmen say, the *climate,* may be
another barrier to expressing ideas, effecting changes, or
simply being heard; children in an emotional state,
overtired, or hungry cannot respond normally, no matter how hard Mother may try to suggest a little picking
up before supper.

The relative status of various members of the family
is part of the communication atmosphere, favorable or
otherwise. The inevitable barrier between parents and
children is not unlike that between supervisor and sub-
ordinate. It is difficult for a child to treat Father as "one
of the boys," no matter how close their relationship may
be. For that matter, no parent really wants to occupy a
position in the family identical to that of his children.
Even though you have tried hard to be a pal to Junior,
he may have justifiable reservations about telling you
all his secrets.

Fear or lack of security may affect the atmosphere in
the home. If children are worried about punishment,
they may be reluctant to tell parents of lost or broken
toys and tools. Or they may fear criticism of things they
do or say to a point where they are afraid to communicate at all. It is up to parents to pay adequate attention
to such fears, and try to maintain an atmosphere which
will invite discussion of new ideas, of things which
might be considered taboo, or even of the most unpleasant subjects. Your child's imagination needs encouragement, not ridicule or criticism.

Most parents have worked out some policy on communication, whether they realize it or not. Their policy

may be, in effect, to have no policy at all; they may wait until the need arises before deciding what to say or do. Such an unsystematic approach, however, can lead to tension and unhappiness. Children like to know about family plans in advance. They prefer to hear good and bad news from their parents rather than from others.

Certain mechanical hurdles must be overcome to insure good communication. These include the lack of facilities in the average home to help jog Father's short memory or that of the preoccupied child. A place to record past and future family activities is essential, such as a calendar or bulletin board. A businesslike approach to keeping track of future dates, meetings, and family events will avert the crisis which may occur when Billy announces at noon that he has been invited to a birthday party at two o'clock. A message pad and pencil left conveniently near the telephone may capture the messages that often escape young minds for hours or days after your return home.

Family communication will also improve if you establish definite times of the week to discuss plans or review school papers. Many business firms rely on a monthly meeting of directors or a weekly departmental meeting for discussion of past and future actions. In the home, similar scheduled meetings may yield dividends.

Choice and use of words constitute a major mechanical hurdle in the family, just as they do in the business world, where much attention has been paid to problems of semantics. Parental suggestions and orders are misinterpreted with infuriating frequency. In *Please Don't*

Eat the Daisies, Jean Kerr quotes her son in a classic example: "Well, if I put *all* my things in the wash, I'll have to put my shoes in and they will certainly break the machinery."

The question of interpreting teen-age jargon is more specialized. It should not be necessary to learn a whole new language in order to understand your children, but only to have an appreciation of the fact that there *are* differences in how various members of the family speak and how they interpret what others say and do.

If there is no clear communication policy, children will often play one parent against the other in an effort to get one to say "yes" when the other has already said "no." Or one parent may block the other to the extent that youngsters feel that they cannot "get through." Some of these situations will arise regardless of what we do, but it should not be difficult to work out a way for Mother and Father to keep in touch with each other. An established chain of command may help. Mother can be the final authority on what clothes to wear, for example, while Father handles the financial questions. An aggravating barrier can be overcome by establishing such channels, as long as they are simple ones, and not formal enough to be frustrating.

A poor choice of time and place for family consultations may be a source of irritation. Orders shouted through the shower curtain do not always make sense or produce the anticipated results. And Junior will not respond well to being asked while he is surrounded by people at the church fair to please do a better job of washing his ears next time.

Some barriers to communication can be avoided entirely with a little thought, while others, already established, can only be overcome through conscious and continuing effort. Mere willingness to communicate is not enough. Someone has to take an active lead in coordinating and controlling the whole process.

Here are three simple pointers which may be used to avoid breakdowns in communication:

1. Encourage a review of what has been said. This involves more than just accepting a direct quotation. Ask for an interpretation of your meaning. You may be surprised at what you get back. Whenever it seems appropriate, encourage a written review. Lists of chores to be done, books to be read, or the itinerary of a trip will be better fixed in young minds if some notes are taken.

2. Invite participation through questions and suggestions. Silence on a child's part may mean merely that he is thinking of something else, not that he understands and agrees with what you have said. Ask him what he thinks and how he feels about your ideas. Make it a two-way conversation, not a monologue.

3. Try to see the other point of view. This is a major requirement which we will touch on in greater detail in subsequent chapters.

Where barriers already exist, they must be identified and analyzed if they are to be overcome. Even after an argument has started, it should be possible to pause long enough to figure out whether the misunderstanding is a result of faulty communication. If you recognize this to be the problem, say so. You will find that taking the blame off the children or your spouse and placing it on a third party, communication, will help ease the stress of the moment. It may even settle the argument.

Review the problem as soon as possible after recognizing its existence. With the barrier already in view, look below the surface facts for the real reason why things went wrong. This will permit not only settling the immediate issue but also seeing how to avoid making the same mistake in the future. Sometimes the analysis of a simple problem will lead to a change in patterns of family behavior that have always been troublesome.

Throughout the process of overcoming communication barriers, it is important to be pleasantly co-operative. A harsh approach may cancel out any benefits to be gained by analyzing the problem. Try to see the other's point of view. Have a broad outlook rather than a narrow or grudging attitude in admitting your own mistakes or accepting the fact that others were wrong. Think of how the three pointers listed above might have been applied, and of what you can now do to improve matters.

In this chapter, we have discussed communication in a general way, together with some of the communication skills which may prove useful in the home. In the chapters which follow we will consider in greater detail such specific communication activities as interviews; giving orders, assignments, and instruction; giving and getting information; discipline and correction; praise, encouragement, and advice.

II

Conducting an Interview

No one could miss the fact that eight-year-old Jeff is tired and cross when he pushes open the front door. His father hears his protesting voice even before he comes into sight, and retreats deeper behind his newspaper. Jeff's protests grow louder as he enters the living room. "Those kids from down the street wrecked our fort! Hey, Dad, you know what? Those jerky kids . . ."

Mother pokes her head in from the kitchen to greet Jeff: "Supper's almost ready, so please wash your hands."

But Jeff is too wound up in his story to hear her. "Listen, Dad, those big kids tore down our fort and we didn't do anything. It's not fair!"

Father emerges briefly. "Well, there's no time to talk about it now. Supper's almost ready. Look at those shoes! You've got mud all over everything."

Jeff takes off his shoes without interrupting his tale of woe. "We just don't think it's fair. Somebody oughta tell those kids . . . who do they think they are, anyway? Think they're such big shots!"

Mother calls again from the kitchen: "Wash your hands, everybody. The potatoes will get cold."

"Listen, Dad. Larry and I had this good fort all built . . ."

Father reappears from behind the paper to interrupt Jeff. "Oh, it was just some old boards, Jeff. You can build it up again tomorrow."

Jeff's voice rises to an indignant squeak. "But it was a good fort! We worked all afternoon on it. They'll just do the same thing again tomorrow." By now Jeff is shouting, and jumping up and down in fury. "They're awful! I hate them!"

The volume forces Father into paying attention. "Well, were you bothering them?"

"No, we weren't. Larry and I were just working away on our fort and along they came. They're always after us."

At this point Jeff's sister Nancy enters. Nancy is twelve, and feels very superior to Jeff and all his problems. "Personally, I don't blame them for being after you. You're always spying on them and wrecking *their* things. How about when you swiped their bench?"

Jeffs turns on her, sputtering. "We did not. You don't know anything. You just like them best, that's all!"

This side issue is too much for Father. "All right, all right. I can't settle these things. You'll just have to

Jerry Marcus, *American Legion Magazine*

"What's the matter with you these days? You used to be
so much fun!"

learn to get along with the other kids, Jeff. Don't come bothering your mother and me with all your squab-bles."

"But it's not fair, Dad! They beat us up all the time, and they're much bigger."

Mother pokes her head in again, but forgets about the pork chops when she hears this remark. "Yes, they are. They really act like bullies. Honestly, Robert, I wish you *would* do something about it."

Growing anxious about his supper, Father hastily re-verses himself. "Okay, Jeff. If they keep it up, you tell them I'll fix them. Now go and get ready for supper!"

This may be the end of the matter for the evening, but you can be sure it is not the last of it. Jeff remains uneasy, dissatisfied over not having really convinced anyone of his position, and knowing that there will be more trouble tomorrow. Mother and Father are a long way from agreeing on the wisdom of parental interfer-ence, and neither one of them has learned enough about this particular incident to know whether such in-terference is warranted. What could have been an ex-cellent opportunity for Jeff to air his grievance, and for one or both of them to advise him on the whole question of neighborhood relations, has been wasted. It really is too bad, particularly when we know that Father would never allow such a thing to happen dur-ing his eight-to-five existence at the department store downtown. He has been trained in interviewing for his work in the Personnel Department there. Is it possible for him to bring some of that training home with him

at five o'clock? We think so. As proof, let us take a look
at the household next door.

Larry Brown is equally tired and cross when he comes
home with a protest identical to Jeff's. His father has
just settled down with the paper, too, as the youthful
voice invades the room.

"Hey, Dad, those big guys down the street broke
down our fort. . . ."

Larry's mother enters: "Supper's almost ready, Larry.
Please wash you hands and get ready."

But here the picture changes as Mr. Brown speaks up.
"Just a second, dear. Larry and I were going to take a
minute or two to talk about the fort, then he'll be
ready. Right, Larry?"

Larry nods; Mother retreats; Mr. Brown looks at
Larry attentively. When Larry resumes the tale of the
damaged fort, his father says nothing until he is finished.

"Well, Larry, that sounds like a tough one to figure
out. I think we ought to talk some more about it. But
let's get supper out of the way first, then we'll really
have time to put our minds to it. Okay with you?"

Larry reluctantly agrees and goes to clean up. When
his mother hears of this arrangement, she promises to
keep his twin sisters out of the way.

From his business experience and training Mr. Brown
has learned some lessons which he finds he can apply
at home. Just as he would never try to settle an office
dispute at ten minutes of five, here he has immediately

—almost automatically—realized that the before-supper interview is not the best time to settle anything. After giving Larry his attention long enough for the boy to blow off steam and tell him the general nature of the problem, he then sets the stage for a constructive discussion when the atmosphere will be more favorable and they can talk without interruption.

After supper, Larry and his father return to the quiet of the living room while Mother and the twins clean up the kitchen. Mr. Brown puts Larry at ease with a casual reference to a picture in the newspaper, and takes a minute to discuss it. Then, with Larry sitting beside him on the couch, he leads off with a question designed to start the boy talking again.

"Now, about the fort, Larry. What happened, anyway?"

Larry starts to talk, and Mr. Brown shows an evident interest in hearing the whole story—no hiding behind the newspaper for him. Food has had a calming effect on Larry. Matter-of-factly he tells of the older boys who knocked down the fort he and Jeff had built out of boards. "They're just a bunch of bullies, Dad. I wish you and Mom would do something." He pauses, looking hopefully at his father.

"You'd like us to do something, Larry." Mr. Brown senses that there is more to the story. He encourages Larry to stop and think about what he is asking by repeating the boy's last words. He then looks expectantly at Larry.

"Well, we're always having trouble. . . ." Larry pauses.

"Trouble? What kind of trouble?"

"Last week they chased us away from their fort. They even threw stones at us." Mr. Brown nods, watching Larry attentively. Larry looks a little sheepish. "We really weren't doing anything. . . ." A pause, with no reply from his father. "Well, not much, anyway." Another pause. "Of course, we did use some of their boards."

"I see."

"Maybe they were trying to get them back. . . ."

"You think that maybe they broke down your fort to get back the boards you took from them?" A leading question from Mr. Brown, who has now had a chance to size up the situation. Larry agrees that this is possible.

"Why don't we all get together tomorrow after I get home and sort out the boards? I'd be glad to help."

By now father and son have reached an agreement on how to solve the problem. Mr. Brown knows from his business experience that using interviewing skills alone does not always provide the complete solution. When the Sales and Shipping Departments are feuding, he uses interviewing skills to get the information he needs, then calls a meeting and acts as mediator in order to reach an agreeable settlement. In the same manner he is now prepared to help settle the neighborhood feud.

DO'S AND DON'TS OF INTERVIEWING

DO'S:

1. *Try to See Both the Immediate and the Long-Term Purpose.* A well-conducted interview can be a means of developing the child. Larry was given an opportunity to blow off steam, while at the same time his father tried to guide him toward a long-term solution of his neighborhood trouble. He also tried to make him realize that it was not wholly a one-sided affair.

2. *Show Interest in a Friendly, Encouraging Manner.* Larry's father took the trouble to put him at ease with some small talk, then opened the discussion with a well-phrased question. This was in direct contrast to Jeff's father, who heard very little of Jeff's report from behind his paper.

3. *Take the Time to Make Advance Preparations.* Know the purpose of your interview; gather as many facts as possible, and set the stage. Postponing the interview until after supper gave Mr. Brown a chance to arrange for a quiet setting and to give Larry's problem a little thought before plunging into a solution.

4. *Listen Actively.* The sequence of Larry's interview with his father shows the value of appropriate listening responses. Without a lengthy interrogation, Mr. Brown got the picture of a two-way squabble over boards between the two groups of boys, and was able to make Larry himself see that it was not all the fault of "the other guys."

5. *Reach an Agreement on the Necessary Action.* It

didn't take long to find a solution after Larry admitted the fact that he and Jeff might have aggravated the other boys. Recognizing that the boys might still run into trouble in trying to settle it the next day, Mr. Brown offered his services. When Larry agreed, the interview was concluded on a constructive note.

DON'TS:

1. *Don't Try to Conduct an Interview Under Unfavorable Conditions.* These conditions may include undue fatigue, or an inappropriate time or place. Jeff's tired and hungry state made it impossible for him to tell his troubles in a reasonable manner. Both the time and place were also inauspicious, with Mother and Nancy both interrupting and supper cooling in the kitchen.

2. *Don't Interrupt.* Even if there had been no outside interruptions, Jeff scarcely had a chance to tell his full story. His father interrupted him with his remarks about muddy shoes, the nature of the fort, and finally to say that he "can't settle these things." Too many interruptions cancel out the value of holding an interview.

3. *Don't Put the Other Person on the Defensive.* Try not to ask questions or make remarks which show lack of sympathy for the other person's point of view. "It was just some old boards" showed Father's lack of understanding of how important the fort was to Jeff, and started him off on another indignant tangent.

4. *Don't Ask Poorly Framed Questions.* Avoid giving the other person a chance to answer *yes* or *no* if you are

interested in drawing out the whole story. "Were you bothering them?" can only lead to a "No!" In contrast, Mr. Brown's query: "What kind of trouble?" opened the door for further discussion.

5. *Don't Conclude the Interview Without Agreeing on a Solution.* Jeff's interview with his father was concluded without accomplishing anything at all either within the family or in terms of neighborhood relations. It is essential for a parent to take the time to listen, and to take an active part in helping solve the problems of his children, as Mr. Brown did. If the two people holding the conversation can agree on a solution, then putting it into action follows naturally and easily.

* * *

By an interview, we mean a purposeful conversation between two people. In this chapter we are concerned for the most part with interviews between parent and child, conducted by the parent. In addition, parents are frequently involved in interviews with teachers, doctors, coaches and counselors concerning their children's progress and welfare. All too often, they leave such an interview feeling baffled and uncertain, realizing too late that they failed to get the information they particularly wanted. Whatever the occasion, the application of some simple techniques may prove helpful.

When a parent conducts an interview with a child, it is especially important for him to have a clear purpose and to prepare for the conversation in a businesslike manner. Such an interview need not be formal, lengthy, or overly serious. It is distinguished from a casual conversation in that it is *purposeful*.

A parent may have in mind any one of several basic purposes when he decides that the time has come to have an interview with one of his children. His long-range objective may be to promote understanding or obtain co-operation for a continuing period of time. A talk of this kind might be held with a child to review his place in the home and his responsibilities to his parents or toward younger children.

Interviews or serious talks may be held periodically to help develop the child. Such conversations might concern preparation for the future in such matters as handling money, making the best use of leisure time, getting along with others, or sportsmanship.

Another long-range objective might be to clarify some new family situation. Explaining the implications of a change in job for Father or the approaching arrival of a new baby should be done through meaningful two-way discussion, and not treated as a casual news item.

Interviews between parent and child may also have more immediate objectives, such as gaining or giving information, or finding out specific facts. Sometimes the use of interviewing skills will quickly determine who broke the neighbor's window; whereas the use of a blunt question or threat would produce only a negative reaction.

An interview may also provide an opportunity for a child to blow off steam. Good interviewing techniques are useful when Junior is anxious to pour out assorted tall tales about his sufferings at the hands of his cruel older sister.

Another common interviewing situation occurs when a parent seeks to give advice or instruction. The immediate objective of teaching Bobby how to drive a nail, for example, or of counseling Linda on teen-age behavior can be accomplished through application of the simple skills described below.

Similarly, a little thought and strategy may provide a more effective remedy for a specific problem than a brusque order and an authoritative manner. If the teen-age daughter's room is so untidy that she cannot find a place to sit down, the immediate need is to get her to straighten it up. At the same time, the young lady can be brought into a discussion of how to prevent such extremes of untidiness in the future. Properly handled, she will not feel rebellious or that she has had a "bawling out" at her advanced age.

We can now see that the home situations in which an interview may be useful are numerous and varied. (Interviews which are chiefly concerned with correcting or disciplining will be discussed in the next chapter.)

Children's grievances cannot be settled by collective bargaining; and yet children, too, deserve a fair hearing, one that is as impartial as the family relationship will allow. A few casual words from Mother or Father cannot adequately settle matters of health, hygiene, safety, allowances, or assigned chores. Even the most difficult and unusual problem can be faced in a parent-child interview if it is approached in a systematic, constructive way.

Of course there are problems in being an effective interviewer just as there are in trying to be a model parent. Emotional crises occur in the most orderly households, and personality clashes cannot always be overcome by the application of theories or techniques. Sometimes it is hard for a parent to appreciate just how badly hurt the six-year-old pride can be, or how much pressure is being put on the twelve-year-old who is taller than all his classmates. Nor is it possible for most parents to keep their own emotions under control at all times. Parents have bad days, too. This is one of the hardest things for children to understand, just as the worker often loses sight of the fact that his boss is only human and has a normal assortment of weaknesses.

Faulty communication due to emotional or other factors can add difficulties to an interview. Misunderstanding may lead to arguments and accusations, and result in a complete breakdown of negotiations.

A little preparation goes a long way in avoiding the difficulties just mentioned. There is no need to meditate for hours before interviewing a child about his performance of some household chore. But some prior thought, and possibly a discussion in advance between his parents, may prove helpful. A lot can also be learned from the experience of others. Find out how your friends approach the ticklish situations which arise with their own children. An occasional exchange of views is a good idea, just as in business the so-called "experience meeting" is used to learn new and improved ways of doing the job.

In preparing for an interview, you should try to have some facts on the topic to be discussed. Try to think in advance of key questions and statements which will start the interview going in the right direction, and keep it on the same track. Know the purpose behind your questions. What do you want to find out, or discuss? What do you hope to accomplish? A close look at your motives in advance will prove worth while.

Another helpful preparation is to set the stage with a thought to timing, privacy and comfort. Otherwise, embarrassment and humiliation may cancel out everything that has been accomplished. Unless you run a military establishment, the child with whom you are talking should not have to stand at attention or even stand at all. It is far better for both of you to relax and be comfortable. Try to arrange it so that there are no interruptions. Make sure that the interview is neither too long nor too short to accomplish its purpose. Use the time to best advantage.

We suggest several steps to create the right atmosphere at the beginning of an interview with your child, and to provide a means of carrying through to a successful conclusion.

1. Without overdoing it, try to have a relaxed, pleasing manner which will put the child at ease. Smile, be friendly, be complimentary whenever appropriate, and show genuine interest. Just because you are having a serious talk does not mean you have to act like an ogre.

Some preliminary small talk may help create a warmer atmosphere than if you jump right into the main topic of conversation.

2. Hear the whole story without interruption. A parent should think of himself as a referee or a judge, not the lawyer for the prosecution. As such he should encourage talk, and above all he should *listen*. Listening is the basic skill of interviewing, and of casual conversation as well. It is so important that we may consider the interviewer to be the *listener*. Many questions need never be asked if the interviewer will listen actively. A parent can quickly detect a child's key thoughts if he will give him the time and freedom to talk without interruptions in the form of questions, orders, or accusations. It is surprising what can be learned from a child if you will only hear him out.

3. Through careful listening, determine the most important ideas, opinions or facts, and try to remember them for future reference. This is particularly important in talking with children, since they are likely to ramble, embroidering their stories to such an extent that only an attentive parent can detect the clues which he must follow up.

4. After hearing the whole story, discuss the relevant points and try to reach an agreement as to what is to be done. Father cannot lean back in his easy chair, grunt, and resume reading the newspaper. Nor should Mother have to step in to suggest that he *do* something. It is up to the interviewer to make sure that an acceptable agreement is reached.

5. As the final step, some kind of decision must be made, whether it is in the form of a reprimand, a suggested course of action, or simply an indication that the conversation is over. Otherwise the purposeful conversation, however skillfully conducted, misses its target.

Throughout an interview there are certain elementary ways of achieving the success which invariably comes to the good listener. As we have indicated, listening is the important part of any rewarding conversation. Most people never stop talking long enough to listen attentively and skillfully. Good listening is a skill in itself, something which can be practiced and improved with conscious effort. Just observe from across the room a person who is known as a good conversationalist, with whom you always enjoy talking. Or watch the woman who has the knack of getting the most reticent man in the party to tell her his life history. They may be saying very little themselves, but through conscious or subconscious effort, they will be doing certain things to promote conversation. They are good listeners who have learned that listening is not a passive activity.

Here are a few things you can do to encourage a child to keep talking. (We realize that this is not always a parent's dearest wish, but sometimes it really is helpful.) To listen actively means to act in such a way that the listener's interest, attention, and readiness to hear more are apparent to the person who is talking. Not wanting to interfere with the speaker's train of thought, the good listener looks interested and remains attentive, but does nothing more until there is a pause in the conversation. Below are listed four specific listening skills which are being taught to foremen and supervisors in business and industry. These skills, practiced in the classroom for use in the shop or office, are equally applicable at home.

1. Interest can be shown when the speaker pauses, by nodding the head slightly or by looking directly at him in a friendly expectant way without saying anything. There is no need to jump in whenever a conversation lags. The speaker may merely wish to catch his breath or collect his thoughts. Frequently a remark at this point will interrupt his train of thought, whereas a quiet pause need not be awkward, and will be less likely to shut off the flow of words. Concentration on keeping your own mouth shut will give you a chance to hear more of what is being said than if you are waiting impatiently to reveal some gem of your own.

2. Sometimes it is more appropriate to say a little something when there is a pause in the conversation than to nod and remain silent. A casual "I see," "Is that so?," "That's right," or any of countless other phrases which we all hear every day will let the speaker know that you are interested in what he has said and in hearing him continue.

3. When children appear to be holding back, a more active participation may be required. Repeating part of what has just been said, usually in the form of a question, may encourage them to go on. When your son says, "Something happened to the stove," it may be better

(assuming that you cannot smell smoke) to appear non-chalant and echo, "The stove?" than to leap to your feet and dash to the kitchen. If the boy is trying to confess that he has scratched the enamel, the calmer response will give him a chance to tell you the whole story.

4. The technique of reflecting back to the speaker your understanding of what he has just said as a means of encouraging him to continue is often referred to as "the mirror." When the eight-year-old says "Johnny just knocked down my castle and it's all his fault!" try coming back with: "You feel it's all his fault" in a matter-of-fact way—unless your small reporter is actually bleeding as a result of the scuffle. Mirroring his statement may give you the rest of the story more quickly than if you shout for Johnny to come downstairs or start asking impatient questions.

Often there is no ready-made opportunity to be a good listener. When you are initiating the interview yourself, you may need a well-thought-out question to get the conversation started. The first query that comes to mind may not be the best way to get a reasonable answer. An impulsive: "Haven't you finished that job yet?" is less likely to produce a successful discussion than: "How is the job coming along?"

There is one conversational skill which is fundamental to success in any type of interviewing situation, just as it is in social conversation. This is the deliberate use of the *open question*, one which cannot be answered "yes" or "no." When a *closed question* is used, we are looking for and should expect a one-word answer which may close the conversation. Our chances for conversational success are increased by using open questions which require something more than a nod or a shake of the head. Start off with *who, what, when, where, which,* or *how* if you want to keep the interview rolling. Most children instinctively prefer to make brief and noncommittal replies, but why encourage them to do so? Surely it is preferable to ask "What did you do when Butch threw the shovel at you?" than "Did you hit him back?"

Questions starting with *is, do, has, can, will,* and similar verbs can effectively stop the flow of information. In A. A. Milne's *Now We Are Six,* Jane, the Good Little Girl, protests that she is always being asked: "Have you been a *good* girl, Jane?" The child wisely questions whether she would be likely to say so if she *had* been bad.

There may seem to be little difference in the effect of open and closed questions when we recall Robert Paul Smith's classic question-and-answer sequence: *Where Did You Go? Out. What Did You Do? Nothing.* Quite so. No approach will work every time, particularly where children are concerned. Our contention is simply that your chances for success in conducting an interview will be better if you ask broad, wide-open questions than if you make it easy for a child to give a one-word answer. At any rate, the use of open questions will test your child's ingenuity.

By now some readers may feel that we are advocating

coddling your child, that this interviewing technique and these ways to be a good listener are too permissive, not forceful enough to be effective. We believe that the assertion of authority does not rely on outshouting the children or roaring around the house to induce fearful submission. We are not advocating a soft approach to every situation, but feel that by thinking before you speak, and by making sure that your child has a chance to give his story before you jump to conclusions, you will reach a mutually satisfactory agreement without sacrificing authority or losing the respect of your child.

III

Correcting Other People

When Joe came home from work tonight he was smiling and happy after putting in a rewarding eight hours at the office. He had influenced, co-operated, communicated, and delegated. He had performed his job according to the best precepts of the management training course he was taking at the college downtown. The ideas of the professor, a man with both a broad business background and a high academic standing, hummed in the back of Joe's mind.

Joe's wife, Barbara, was in a good mood too. She had waxed the kitchen floor, made a pie, and still found time to put her feet up after lunch and read a magazine. All had gone well that day, with one exception: the boys' report cards seemed to require some discussion concerning certain black marks imposed by the teachers.

Joe walks into the kitchen to greet the youngsters who are having an early supper. As he looks around the room he scowls, and his office personality inexplicably vanishes.

"Mike, did you spill that milk on the floor?"

"No."

"Well, who did?"

"I don't know. Bob was pouring."

"Bob, did you?"

"Yeh."

Rising inflection: "Why didn't you mop it up, then?"

"Let Mike do it. He was the one who wanted more. These darned bottles always spill when they're full."

"Well, if you boys can't be more careful . . ."

And so it goes. What might have been a helpful discussion of how to pour milk and an easy approach to getting it cleaned up becomes a frustrating Gestapo interrogation which only leaves everybody annoyed.

After Joe and Barbara have had their dinner the time comes to discuss report cards. Bob comes first. He has a D in fifth-grade arithmetic.

"Bob, this certainly isn't too good a report. Your arithmetic is very bad. You know, both Mother and I were real sharks at this when we were in school. What's the matter with you?"

"I don't know."

"Did the teacher tell you it was this bad?"

"Nope."

"Did you turn in all your homework papers?"

"Sure."

Joe doesn't seem to be doing too well.

"Did she give the others marks like this?"

"I don't know."

Joe is getting a bit desperate. He really wants to help
Bob, wants him to do better, but he seems to be up
against a stone wall. Like some blundering animal, he
tries to batter his way through. On he goes, in a harsher
tone: "For goodness sake, then, what *was* the matter?
There has to be some reason for this D. Did you sass
the teacher or something?"

"No." Bob cannot answer two questions at once. The
one-word reply seems the easiest way out. By this time
he is uncomfortable and worried about possible disciplinary action, but also aware that his father may just
give up. Figuring that he may escape if the interview
does not last too long, he volunteers nothing.

"Well, you'd better bring this mark up next month
or I'll have to go down to school and talk to your
teacher. Maybe she should give you more homework,
or keep you after school until you improve." (Joe is
always saying things like this to the boys—never does
much.)

Joe cannot understand why Bob has failed to get a
decent mark in arithmetic. That should be an easy subject. It seems too bad that his boy doesn't make the
grade. Bob sidles toward the door.

"Okay, go ahead. At least you got a few good marks."

Bob brightens, but the interview is over with this
belated compliment. He thinks he might as well take

the crumb of praise and run rather than risk more abuse.

Now Mike is summoned. The office humanitarian by this time is in no mood for the soft approach. *These boys have got to learn the importance of good marks, and, by heaven, I'll impress them with this if it's the last thing I do.*

"Mike!" (normal tone).

"Mike!!!!" (thirty decibels).

"Yes, Dad?"

"Come in here. I want to talk to you about your report card."

(Wait a bit, Joe. Who's supposed to be talking? And who is supposed to want to hear about that report card?)

There follows a repetition of the discussion with Bob. The reason why their children should be getting unsatisfactory marks remains a mystery. Joe and Barbara speculate about it after Mike departs. They decide that both boys must now realize the importance of good marks. (Because of Joe's tone of voice?) The next time the boys will surely do better. (Solely on the basis of being told to?) *And, anyway, the teachers probably don't understand them.*

Now let us watch and listen at the office as Joe, an assistant accountant, arrives the next morning. Report cards are forgotten, but there is a report on Joe's desk. The home office has returned it with a curt note from the Chief Accountant himself which in no way makes Joe appear to be the next branch manager. Joe gulps a few times in anger as he realizes that this is the report compiled by Arlene Smith, one of his most reliable girls. *She really should have known better!* He sends a message for her to come into his cubicle.

So far, the drama is like that of Bob and Mike. But wait! Is this our Joe?

"Thanks for coming so promptly, Arlene. Perhaps you can help me fix up this report that came back this morning." He hands it to her, with its attached note.

As Arlene reads the criticism from the Chief Accountant a look of dismay comes over her face. "Oh, Mr. Jones, that's the report I did. I'm awfully sorry."

"Now, Arlene, don't worry about it. You're one of our best people and one little mistake isn't going to change my opinion of your work. Let's see if we can fix it up and get it back to General Bookkeeping by return mail. What did happen, anyway?"

Arlene sighs with relief. "Oh, Mr. Jones, thank you. I was afraid you'd want to fire me or something!" (Maybe he did want to at the moment, but what good would that do?) "You see, I sent that out the day you were away last week. The boss was called out suddenly and there was no one to give it a final look. But it was due and I thought it really should go out."

Joe nods sympathetically.

Arlene rushes on: "I guess I really should have run the figures off on the comptometer a second time, but I thought I had everything straightened out. And then Jane went home sick and I had to finish up her stuff. . . . Oh, dear, I do hope we're not in bad with the home office!"

"Now, don't worry. Why don't you fix this up the way you think it should be? The only problem I see, Arlene, is how we can avoid this in the future. What ideas do you have about that?"

"Maybe we should schedule this report for a day earlier each month, Mr. Jones. Then either you or the boss is bound to be here to check it. But don't worry, I'm going to be more careful next time, *before* you see it!"

The comparison between this interview and the ones Joe had with Bob and Mike is all too obvious. It never occurred to him to apply at home anything he had learned in his training course lecture on "Correcting Others." Below are listed a few hints which might have been of some help to him when he talked to his boys.

DO'S AND DON'TS OF
CORRECTIVE INTERVIEWS

First and Foremost DO: *Forget the Past Except as it Affects the Future.*

DO'S:

1. *Take a Positive Approach.* Try to *clarify* and *correct*. If at all possible, compliment before you critcize. Both of Joe's report-card interviews would have been off to a far better start if he had opened up with a comment on Bob's and Mike's good marks; and then gone

on to see how they could raise the bad ones to match. Note that in his office he takes the time to thank Arlene Smith for her prompt arrival before getting down to their less pleasant business of correcting her report and figuring out how to avoid such errors in the future.

2. *Be Sure the Purpose Is Broad Enough.* Try to find out what happened; get it fixed; and see how to avoid future trouble. If possible, try to clarify the whole situation through the specific example. Be sure that your criticisms are primarily a means to an end, that they are aimed at future development and progress. Making Arlene redo the incorrect report didn't satisfy Joe, just as raising Bob's arithmetic mark from a D to a C would not really be enough. At home as in business, it's important to consider how you can affect the future by correcting a previously made mistake.

3. *Make Sure Both People Understand the Error.* The person making the correction should take the time and trouble to help the one at fault see what's wrong. Certainly Arlene realized what she had done and why it was a serious matter. Do Bob and Mike know why their parents want them to improve their marks? Is it only to make them live up to Joe's and Barbara's own scholastic records? A little general explanation of the importance of good study habits would go a long way at this point.

4. *Listen Actively and Keep an Open Mind.* Joe was so busy talking and letting off steam over a couple of bad marks that he never did bother to draw out Bob or Mike. And yet in his office he let Arlene give him her

whole version of how the error had taken place. Somehow he even managed to be sympathetic although his own career may have been damaged by her carelessness. That is all part of the science of human relations. He has learned about that. All he needs to do now is to apply this knowledge at home.

DON'TS:

1. *Don't Just Blame and Scold.* Criticism alone is not enough. Joe's little talks with Bob and Mike leave them on the defensive, thoroughly uncomfortable, and without any idea of how to improve, whereas in the office, Joe and Arlene Smith together have agreed on a procedure: a new schedule which should improve matters in the future.

2. *Don't Stop at Getting the Error Corrected.* That is only the beginning. In the spilled-milk episode, both Bob and Mike could have profited by a short discussion of how to hold a full milk bottle. Arlene was more than happy to put her mind to the problem when Joe asked her: "How can we avoid this in the future?"

3. *Don't Guess at What Happened.* It's important to get the facts, either from the person at fault or from outside sources. Wouldn't it have been better for Joe or Barbara to consult Bob's teacher before passing judgment, since Bob didn't seem to understand why he got that D? In Arlene's case, Joe is able to get the facts about the incorrect report both from the home office and directly from her.

4. *Don't Let a Single Mistake Affect a Person's Stand-*

ing. To keep proper perspective, past performance should always be considered in judging an error. It's entirely possible that Bob never had a D before. He's upset too. A more understanding approach from his father with a review of past good marks seems only fair, and would be more encouraging than a bawling out. Certainly Joe was quick to assure Arlene that "one little mistake" isn't going to change his opinion of her work or of her value to the company. His own sons might appreciate such an assurance.

Note: Additional DO'S AND DON'TS can be found in Chapter II on interviewing in general.

*   *   *

In the previous chapter we described techniques for use in day-to-day interviewing situations. We mentioned ways to create the proper atmosphere for a purposeful conversation with a child, and specific skills which can be used to save time, effort, and parental sanity. Because we regard discipline as one of the most difficult problems parents have to face, we now want to discuss in detail the *corrective interview*.

By corrective interview we mean a purposeful conversation between parent and child which is held primarily to correct or reprimand. The interview is specifically directed toward correcting a mistake or improving a general situation which is disturbing the family harmony. It is not our purpose to decide for the parents whether to take positive action with the birch rod or razor strop. We merely suggest that any situation which might involve punishment, drastic or otherwise, should be analyzed and discussed by both parent and child in a well-conducted corrective interview. Only in this way can they arrive at a reasonable course of action which is agreeable to both.

We want to emphasize as strongly as possible the need for a clear purpose in the corrective interview. Ordinarily there are several objectives which the parent should have in mind when the time comes to assume the stern role of disciplinarian. It is important to look at the broad picture of what you hope to accomplish before telling Junior that you want to have "a little talk."

Certainly if a youngster has stopped up the overflow in the washbasin and left the water running, the first thing to do is to turn off the water and mop up. *First* get things fixed: staunch the flow of blood; remove the matches from the tiny hands. But after that is accomplished, do not stop with a slap or a harsh word if you really wish to correct the child.

The second objective of the corrective interview is to find out exactly what happened. Try to get the facts by using the skills discussed in the previous chapter on interviewing. Do not jump to conclusions—or even jump up and down—until you know what really did occur. Instead of guessing how the little boy got into trouble, give him time to cool off so that he can give you his story. In the meantime you can be cooling off too. Once you have learned what appears to be the full story you are in a much better position to judge how to guide the discussion further and to decide upon what action is needed.

After a confession has been made or the misdeed acknowledged, it is usually not difficult to proceed to the next step, which is to reach some agreement on how to avoid similar trouble in the future. We are assuming that the lessons of Chapter I have been learned, and that the parent is not dominating the conversation during this step. He tries to make sure that the child has learned his lesson from the situation, and guides him to talk in terms of future action. The less said by Father or Mother at this stage the better, although the child may need some help in expressing his ideas and in working them out in a constructive way.

A further purpose to have in mind when faced with the necessity for remedying a bad situation is to conclude the interview with a clarification of the whole situation of which the misdeed may be only one part. The child's duties or responsibilities, his place in the family, school, or neighborhood could be reviewed at such a time. The discussion could serve to emphasize the wrongdoing or poor judgment, and point the way to better future behavior.

With your purpose firmly in mind, it is important to make sure that your approach to the child who has done wrong is positive. It is not necessary to rant and rave about everything that is bad or wrong. Many times there will be good things to talk about as well as items for correction, high marks as well as low ones on the report card. If possible, try to compliment before you criticize.

The corrective interview should not be just an opportunity for a parent to blame and scold. Properly handled, it should preclude the necessity for a lot of harsh words, and lessen the irritations of both parent and child. Over thirty years ago, Mary P. Follett, a leader in the field of industrial human relations in England, said that we should not blame for the sake of blaming but should make what we have to say accomplish something. A parent's words of wisdom should be uttered in such a way, at such a time and under such circumstances as to be part of his child's education, not just punishment.

A positive approach to correction attempts to correct the action, not just criticize the individual. If you are always looking for someone to blame, you are losing sight of your true purpose as a parent, which is to correct, to educate, and to develop your child. The successful parent, like the business manager who is successful in dealing with people, does not use authority as a weapon for criticism and faultfinding, nor does he expect to be followed and obeyed because of his supervisory position. Rather he tries to arouse a feeling of co-operation, of mutual interest in common ends. The correction of mistakes can be treated as a positive way toward a happier coexistence.

It is necessary to keep the background in mind when deciding on corrective action. The parent must think in terms of the children involved, their past performances and past relationships. Good or bad, these factors must all be taken into account in deciding what to do. The boy who tips over the canoe the first time out should not get quite the same treatment as the youth with a lot of canoeing experience who tips it over because of carelessness.

Both child and parent must understand from as nearly a common point of view as possible just what was involved. Was the mistake apparent at the time? To the experienced parent the consequences of playing with the emergency brake are obvious, but perhaps not so to a four-year-old. The innate ability to see things through our children's eyes in something few of us possess, but the more we try to do so the more successful we will be in our dealings with them.

A similar barrier to correcting children successfully is built by the parent who fails to make sure that the errant child has had an opportunity to see and understand his mistake. The parent should take the time and trouble to make sure that there is no question as to the nature of the misdeed and its consequences. The five-year-old terror who thinks it is fun to light matches can quickly see his mistake, or feel the results of it. But his background is probably too limited for him to appreciate without explanation the subtler implications of throwing his food around the kitchen or refusing to help pick up his toys. Explaining the thought underlying your corrective action in the latter case may be more involved than that required on the way to the doctor's office with a burned hand.

In the corrective interview it is particularly important to listen carefully and actively. The listening skills discussed in Chapter II are especially useful in an interview of this kind. In addition to saying as little as possible, it is essential to keep an open mind. This type of parent-child conversation may be charged with emotion due to the direct effect of the mistake. The fact that the living-room rug has been stained with grape juice, or Mother's new scarf returned torn from a teen-age bowling party, may make it difficult to assess any but the more obvious facts. Sometimes, however, clear consideration of the facts, with whatever objectivity the moment will allow, may reveal that the boy next door was the one who spilled the grape juice and fled, leaving your own child as the apparent criminal. Or you may suddenly recall that you yourself suggested wearing the new scarf, or learn that the tear was not after all a result of carelessness.

The interviewer must also try to keep the problem in its proper perspective. The big dramatic scene, the long-term threats, the cold reception, should not be indiscriminately used. After the child appreciates the mistake, try to see how he must view it in relation to his total existence. Do not magnify small errors out of all proportion. Try to save your severe approach for the most serious matters.

Through the use of open questions and proper listening responses as discussed earlier, and with pursuit and follow-up of the child's key thoughts, it should be possible to reach a satisfactory conclusion as to what action is necessary. Your attention and interest in hearing the whole story and in encouraging the child to take part in the decision should go a long way toward convincing him that he has had a fair hearing. Carrying out the action agreed on should then become less painful than if a more abrupt approach had been used throughout the corrective interview.

Drawing by Stan Hunt, © 1958 The New Yorker Magazine, Inc.

"Jim, you must stop referring to the children as personnel."

IV

Giving Orders and Assignments

At TEN O'CLOCK on an October Saturday, Harry, who is not ordinarily a Heavy Father, decides that this is the weekend to clean out the garage.

"We're going to get those kids to work today," he informs his wife Fran as he drains his morning coffee. "That garage is a mess."

His three children pick this moment to troop through the room on their way outdoors. They are: Linda, thirteen; Henry, ten; and Jimmy, who is not quite seven.

"Hey, kids!" They pause, fidgeting, only half listening. "The garage is a mess. Nobody's done anything about it all summer. I want it cleaned up today, d'you hear?"

The children, already in motion, reply simultaneously:

"Sure."

"Okay, Pop."

"Mmm."

They are all headed in different directions: Linda to walk uptown and look over the latest rock 'n' roll records; Henry to build a tree house with Willie; Jimmy to set up Fort Laramie in the sandbox next door. Harry's words have not penetrated these well-formed plans.

Half an hour later Harry leaves to do the weekend errands. He grumbles as he trips over the hose while getting into the car. No children in view. Uptown he has to wait forty-five minutes to get a dog license, and after delays both at the hardware store and the gas station he nearly misses the noon deadline at the Post Office. Morning gone; temper thin. The only change on the home-and-garage front is that a bicycle has been moved out to block the driveway.

Fran has just finished her morning stint of housework, and is now ready to sit down and consider the pleasanter aspects of the weekend plans. Harry's greeting is not quite what she is hoping to hear. "Where are the kids? Why haven't they cleaned up the garage?"

Fran has been busy. She wants to sit down. "I'm sure *I* don't know. They went out."

"Well, I'm going to find them and put them to work. The whole morning's wasted. Nothing's been done."

"But Harry, it's almost lunchtime."

Harry explodes, and Fran returns to the kitchen to slap sandwiches together. When she calls the children

"The Budgetleys" by Bram, *Christian Science Monitor*

"A warm Saturday comes along and he wants to tidy up the whole wide world."

for lunch, they appear instantly, diverted from their morning activities by the prospect of food.

Harry greets them with a roar: "Now look here, that garage looks wonderful, doesn't it?" Blank stares and silence all round.

"Well, did you clean it up as I asked?"

One "Nope" and two negative shakes of the head.

Fran intervenes as Harry prepares to explode again, thrusting sandwiches and milk at everyone. Harry gulps his, inviting indigestion. The twenty-minute truce and general refueling help a little.

After lunch, Harry herds the children into the offending garage. "Now! No one leaves until this garage is cleaned up good and proper, understand? It's a pigpen!"

The children open their mouths to protest, but Harry interrupts. "No more nonsense. This job has got to be done right now. At ten o'clock this morning I told you to clean up the garage and now you're going to do it. Everybody get busy. Look at the place. What a mess!" He kicks the hose.

"I didn't do it."

"Jimmy left all those sticks."

"I did not! It was Larry."

Harry roars again. "I don't care who did it! You kids get busy. Pile up the wood. Pick up the toys. Sweep the floor. Take the stuff we don't need down cellar. Get going!" He starts out the door. (How's that again, Harry? Who does what? And why?)

Linda and Henry begin to fight over the only broom.

"Sweep the floor" was the only clear-cut order either one of them heard. Jimmy starts to roll an old tire around the garage, bumping into the other two.

Let us cut the scene here. The garage-cleaning project dissolves into noisy chaos. Within ten minutes Henry has been banished to his room in a tantrum; Jimmy has managed to sneak away while no one was looking; and Linda is left alone in the garage. As she sweeps the dirt from side to side she grumbles self-righteously that "nobody around this place does any work except me." Fran has taken some mending to her room to keep out of it.

Finally Harry gives up and turns on the television; but his mind is not on the ball game. *Those kids ought to be doing more work around here,* he tells himself. *They don't seem to have any sense of responsibility. How are they ever going to learn, anyway? Guess I must be a lousy father.*

What went wrong?

As proof that Harry is neither an ogre nor a bumbling failure at getting along with people, let us see how he handled a comparable situation at his office recently. The assignment he gave his office staff was not too different from the one he gave his children. He asked them to clean out all files and supply cabinets in time for the annual inventory. But note the difference in Harry's approach.

Harry really does know how to give orders. He has had training in this sort of thing. First of all, he set ten o'clock as the most convenient time for everyone to meet, knowing that their urgent early-morning jobs

would be out of the way by then. Visualize the scene
in Harry's office: all are comfortably seated, including
Harry and his secretary, who is ready to take notes on
whatever is decided. Harry introduces the assignment
by explaining why the clean-up job has to be done now,
at the height of their busy season. Next he reviews the
time sequence: when to expect the auditors; when the
inventory will start; and when each portion of the job
should be completed. Everyone is invited to make suggestions as to how and when the work can best be fitted
into the daily routine.

When the group has had a chance to discuss the general picture, Harry gets down to specific details. He
makes sure that the jobs are evenly distributed. Knowing that his secretary is likely to take too much of the
work on herself, he is careful to spell out exactly what
he wants her to do and where her responsibility ends.
He welcomes suggestions from the group as to the nature of each one's task, and asks whether anyone will
need extra help. In conclusion, Harry asks his secretary
to read back the assignments they have agreed on, and
provides for a follow-up: "When each of you has finished, why don't you check in with me and we'll see
how the whole thing is coming along."

All of this has consumed less than half an hour of
office time for Harry and his staff, and a major project
is smoothly and effectively launched. Are there any
parallels between what Harry did at the office and did
not do at home? Outlined below are some of the pros
and cons of giving assignments and orders that Harry

has learned in a management development training course. A brief review may reveal more than one pointer that he could well have used at home.

DO'S AND DON'TS OF
ORDERS AND ASSIGNMENTS

DO'S:

1. *Make the Assignment Specific and Clear-cut.* Spell it out as carefully as possible. Specify: *when* (the time to start and the deadline for completion); *how* (what means are available); *who* (in giving orders to a group); and *what* (the exact limits of the job—what is included and what is not).

2. *Choose a Convenient Time and Place.* Harry called his staff meeting early in the business day, when each member was ready for business but not yet embarked on an important project of his own. At the office he knows better than to start a job just before lunch, as he tried to do at home. He has also learned that it is far more convenient to meet in his office than to try to catch each person going through the hall.

3. *Make the Assignment Detailed.* Be sure to supply enough details. If in doubt, add a few. Harry's "today" was too vague a deadline to mean anything to his children, just as his haphazard orders as to what the children were to do left them all confused.

4. *Provide Proper Motivation.* Try to explain *why* the job has to be done. In Harry's office, it was to get ready for the annual inventory, an objective which was

of interest and value to all the staff. How much better it would have been to awaken his children's interest by explaining that with winter coming they would all be better off with more space in the garage for firewood, sleds and snow shovels. His "do-as-you-are-told" approach led only to resentment and poor performance.

5. *Provide a Follow-up*. Make it simple, concrete, and if possible built into the assignment itself. Once you have assigned a job, don't just go off as Harry did and expect to find it done on your return from uptown. You will do much better with a follow-up of the kind he suggested in the office, whether it is on an hourly, weekly, or even yearly basis.

DON'TS:

1. *Don't Interrupt Plans Already Made*. In particular, do not interrupt with a job that could just as well be done at another time, or with a less important task than the one you are interrupting. The children would have been far more willing to work in the garage if Harry had proposed it before they had made commitments to their friends and formed their plans for the day.

2. *Don't Overload the Most Willing*. Avoid making a workhorse out of the good-natured member of the group. Try to analyze carefully which person is best qualified for the job. Note that Harry distributed the work load so as not to overload his willing secretary. Linda would undoubtedly have appreciated similar treatment at home.

3. *Don't Just Tell Each Person What to Do.* One may much prefer to sweep and another to pile the wood. Let them discuss the division of labor. You may still have to arbitrate if they cannot agree, but Harry's office experiences show that it is more effective to let each person have some say in the arrangements.

4. *Don't Give an Assignment in a Hurry.* Try to present the full picture in a leisurely way. Take the time to speak distinctly, and to explain each step in detail. This is time well spent, as Harry recognized in his office conference. Hurry and tension lead to misunderstanding and a feeling of "How's that again?"

5. *Don't Take a Negative Approach.* Harry's children were immediately on the defensive at his remarks that the garage was a mess, a pigpen, and that nobody had done anything about it all summer. Whenever possible, put your assignment on a "let's do . . ." basis.

* * *

In Chapter I we talked in a general way about communication. Now let us look at a particular aspect of communication in the home which we feel is important enough to merit special attention. Every day finds us ordering and guiding our children, with directions ranging from the brief suggestion that Jimmy hang up his jacket to the detailed instructions needed to prepare his older brother for the job of painting the garage.

In trying to get children to do things, we often fail dismally and wonder why. Businessmen and human-relations specialists have investigated the nature of orders and assignments, and suggest various pointers to help a supervisor make sure that his subordinates will carry out his directions. Application of these skills to any home situation which involves asking children to do even the simplest task may make the difference between successful completion of the assignment and total failure.

We shudder at the picture of the tearful scene which results from a neglected order or a sloppy, half-finished assignment. Let us review the factors which may have led up to such a situation: Father's rising tone of voice when he asked Susie for the fourth time to pick up her room; Mother's emotional and hasty directions for some distasteful kitchen job which is destined never to be completed. There may be many reasons why such orders are never carried out. Some advance preparation is essential for giving any order or assignment. This may require only a few seconds' thought in the case of a routine request like asking the eldest daughter to set the table for supper. Or it may be necessary to think seriously about which chores can be assigned to each child as part of a full day's clean-up project.

One problem which husband and wife may encounter in giving orders to their children is duplication or conflict in their instructions. Duplication is not too serious a problem except for the irritation it may produce in a child who is asked by Father to do the very same chore he is just finishing up for Mother. But even worse is the confusion which results when a child is ordered to do two different things at once. His parents certainly cannot expect to get either job done as directed. And a still more serious aspect is the conflict produced in the child. The younger he is, the more difficult this conflict is to resolve.

Parents do not give conflicting assignments to their children on purpose. They merely fail to take the time to find out whether the child is available. Any youngster is likely to be annoyed at being asked to interrupt his play to do some household chore, but he learns that sometimes it is necessary. However, he may regard it as the final straw to be told to do something else when, willingly or grudgingly, he is in the midst of working for the family good. It is really little wonder that children find parents a bit demanding at times.

It may be necessary to establish a chain of command in the family to make sure that orders emanate from one person only. A simpler suggestion is to have Father check with Mother before blithely ordering Sally to stop whatever she is doing and fetch his pipe. Picture Sally's mental reaction: *You mean stop wiping the dishes, Dad? Now that Mother has finally persuaded me to do them after all that coaxing? How confusing! How delightful!*

Before making an assignment, parents should also think carefully about which child is best qualified to carry it out. Avoid overloading the most willing; and try to encourage inexperienced hands to perform new tasks. In business we hear a lot about "bringing along the future managers." And yet we often forget this principle at home when we continually choose the same child for a particular job.

In introducing an assignment, some thought should also be given to its importance in relation to the time and place. It may be better to wait until the hungry birds have been fed before suggesting a flight from the nest. Many jobs could wait until morning, or at least until after a full meal has relieved normal juvenile fatigue. The fact that a parent *wants* something done now does not necessarily mean that it really *has* to be done now. A slight postponement may be mutually beneficial. We suggest that the commander-in-chief of the household will get better results without relinquishing any parental authority if he does not boom out his commands at a time when there is little hope for peaceful obedience.

Try not to interrupt an important job to assign a minor task. We have already mentioned conflicting orders, in a case where two people are involved in making assignments. Now we refer to the situation wherein Johnny is asked to stop washing the car for a minute to take the hammer in to Father. His father should be happy enough to have the car washed for him without interrupting the job with such a minor request.

In any assignment which is more than a routine minor request a child should be permitted to speak his piece about the job. His suggestions and ideas about what he is to do and how to do it should be encouraged with something more than a snappy: "Any questions?" after the parent has finished talking. Be sure the child is given an opportunity to contribute all he wishes without being shut off or ignored.

If you cannot give orders and assignments in a leisurely, relaxed manner it is probably better not to
bother to give them at all. When you talk too fast, or
mumble, or give your child the impression that you are
in a great rush, he will find it hard to understand what
you expect of him. Stress and tension may lead to re-
sistance. If Mother is delayed for her appointment at
the hairdresser by some frustrating problem of home
or child care, she may issue a series of rapid-fire orders
to the household at large. Older children may well
figure that she won't remember her directions anyway,
so why bother? The younger ones may just stand
rooted, wondering why Mommy is flying around so. In
either case, it is unlikely that her orders will be carried
out.

The assignment itself should be specific and clear-
cut. Do not underestimate how important it is for everyone to have a full understanding of what is involved.
If you are dealing with more than one child, the limits
of the responsibility of each one should be carefully defined.

A vague, haphazard order will not advance the family cause at all. Try to use words that children understand, and above all do not take too much for granted
when you ask a child to do something for you. Consider each child's capacity in order to determine how
much instruction he will need. To insure complete understanding, assignments should include specific built-in
explanations of *what, when,* and *how.* Both the means

of accomplishment and the time for completion, or deadline, should be carefully outlined.

It is better to give too much detail than too little. The time spent in discussing with your teen-age daughter just how she is to prepare the evening meal in your absence is well justified if it keeps the younger children from going hungry. On the other hand, too much repetition of details can be distracting and tiresome. The same daughter will lose all interest in cooking if you tell her three or four times how long to boil water. Use judgment in deciding how much detail your order requires. Probably you will have to spend more time with younger children; but regardless of age, take into account their capacities and experience in determining how much to tell them.

Assignments should be based on a positive approach. "Let's pick up the living room before you go out" is more likely to get favorable attention than "Don't go out and leave that mess in the living room!" It is entirely possible that neither approach will work, and you may have to resort to mental and/or physical torture in the end to get the room picked up at all. But certainly there is more chance of success if the order does not carry in its word or tone any accusation, direct or implied.

The importance of proper motivation should be evident. There is a fundamental distinction between the do-as-you-are-told approach and the attitude of the parents who make sure that their children understand the *why* of their orders. We want a child not only to be willing to do the job, but also to appreciate the reasons for wanting to do it beyond the mere fact of a parental threat or order. Of course, even the best-motivated approach may occasionally backfire too, as in the case of the child who asked indignantly as the guests drove off: "Why did we pick up the living room? They didn't even sit down!"

When the motivation is built into an assignment, children will accept the job more readily and do it in a happier frame of mind. Resentment and misunderstanding can be eliminated if everyone is given a chance to discuss the values and effects of performing the task at hand. A lengthy conference should not be necessary every time a child is given a minor assignment, but a brief explicit discussion should be held whenever the *why* is not readily apparent.

The follow-up or control of an assignment assures not only that the work gets done but also that no serious problems are encountered along the way and that the workers know the supervisor is solidly behind them. The parent or supervisor should also show that he is interested in the effort being made, and pleased with the attitude and accomplishments of all.

Not much success can be expected if an order is given without the promise of help if needed, or some indication that an occasional check-up will be made to see how things are going. Such control does not have to be complicated or time-consuming. It can be as simple as: "When you are through, call me and we'll go over it together." The long-term assignment may require a day-to-day display of interest by the parent, and a difficult mechanical job may involve constant supervision. In such cases, try to keep in mind the precepts of Chapter V on delegation as you hang over the youthful shoulder.

The successful assignment relies on advance preparation; a positive approach; a clear-cut, well-defined purpose; proper motivation; and adequate control or follow-up. The application of any single one of these will improve your chances for success. And the more of them you can apply the better off you will be.

V

Getting Things Done Through Others:
Delegation

MOTHER AND FATHER and the children are all excited. At last they have a chance to leave the city for a real vacation. It certainly was good of Cousin Sue to invite them to use her shore cottage during Father's two-week vacation. And so the family team swings into action.

Team? Let's take another look.

Mother has been working all week, pressing and mending the children's clothes and packing them neatly into suitcases and boxes. Father is now preparing to load them into the car. And where are Susie and Johnny? They have been sent outdoors to play—anything to keep them out from underfoot. For, as Father told himself during his twelfth frantic dash upstairs, *We want to be absolutely sure everything is all set. We'll check and double check on everything ourselves. The kids are too excited to be any help.*

The children are excited, all right. Suddenly they appear, firing questions at Mother.

"When do we leave?"

"May I take my doll buggy?"

"Where's my suitcase?"

"Shall I put in my old blue hat?"

"Can I pack my fish pole?"

"No, no! Susie, Johnny, don't be silly. I've put everything you can possibly use in this big old duffel bag of your father's." (Everything? Just wait until morning!)

A few protests:

"Gee, I wanted to pack my own suitcase!"

"What'll I do with my fish pole?"

Mother is trying to do all the last-minute things at once. She gives Johnny a job to get him out of the way again. "Why don't you get together whatever the cat will need while he's staying next door?" Johnny, pleased, dashes off. A minute later Mother's voice overtakes him:

"Johnny, have you got the cat's bed?"

"Right here."

"Be careful not to spill his sandbox."

"Okay."

"And don't forget Kitty!"

By this time Johnny is thoroughly exasperated. He is ten years old—he knows what the cat needs. *What's the use of helping around here anyway?* He gives up;

disappears. Meanwhile Father is down at the curb, almost through with packing the car. "Everybody ready?" he calls.

Mother is nowhere near ready. There is the lunch to pack, and the notes to write. "Susie, you'll have to write down the phone number for the Browns."

Susie is only six, and not very good at this. "What number? What'll I use? Where is it?" and, finally, "Is this all right?"

"Oh no, for pity sake! That's the Browns' own number. Honestly, you're no help at all! Can't you get anything right? Here, I'll do it. You get in the car. Where's your brother?"

Johnny reappears, cobwebby. He has been looking in the storeroom for some old comics. Mother takes one look and groans. "Here, get Susie into the car and stay there till we're ready."

Johnny grabs Susie by the arm and pulls her out the door, obviously relishing the opportunity to boss his younger sister. As he tries to shove her into the car, she balks. He slaps her. She bites him. Both are howling when Father comes to tear them apart.

"You kids stop fighting or we don't go, you hear?" (Classic parental threat. Do you really mean it, Father?)

The fight is somehow ended, and Father (who *didn't* really mean it) returns to the house for a final check. As he rushes around slamming windows, Mother appears in hat and gloves, at last ready to embark. Father growls at her: "Don't see why I have to do all this.

Can't you get those kids to help?" Mother walks straight on thought without comment.

And so we are off to the shore with the children sulking in the back seat and a gray silence in front. Does it have to be this way? Not necessarily.

At the plant, Father is known as an unusually able administrator. He seems to have time for everything. With everyone but his own family, it is all very simple. Teamwork is what counts, he has learned. He would never let qualified men stand by while he performed the easy tasks. Distribute the work? Of course, that's second nature. Get everyone aboard; make them feel like part of the team—that's right out of Father's speech to the Foremen's Club last month.

Consider an important project that Father had to direct last week: installing a new finishing machine, and fitting it into the over-all manufacturing process. He will not be running the machine himself, nor even checking up every day on the man who does. But it *is* his job to see that the whole new operation runs smoothly. How much of the installation job did he take over himself? How much did he delegate to others?

Let's take a look over his shoulder at about two o'clock Monday afternoon. The new machine is in its proper place, and appears to be in good working order. This is the first time Father has been on the scene since early this morning when he inspected the uncrated machine along with Fred, Finishing Room foreman. Although Fred had never undertaken anything like this before, Father had enough confidence in him to turn over the responsibility for installing the machine. He knew that Fred would closely watch the workmen who were doing the actual bolting down. Never fear, Fred has been trained not to let anyone fool around with a sledgehammer on a delicate machine like this. All morning Father resisted the impulse to hang over Fred's shoulder while the machine was being installed. Instead, he used the time to do his own work, knowing that Fred would let him know if anything went wrong.

Finally, half an hour ago Fred called: "Guess we're all set, Dan. Like to watch the first run through?"

When Father arrives on the scene both Fred and Mac, the newly trained machine operator, greet him with beams and handshakes. All three men are proud of "our" new machine, and interested in its performance, each from a different point of view. Now that it has been ordered, delivered, installed, and made ready to roll, the actual operation will be up to Mac. Fred is Mac's direct supervisor, responsible for all the work in the Finishing Room. But both Fred and Mac know where to go if it should appear that the machine is not going to pay its way; or if there are signs of any serious mechanical trouble that they cannot handle. Straight to Father. As Production Manager, he knows when to step in and when to leave his men alone.

Mac may make a mistake or two on the first few runs. That is all part of learning the job and becoming a more skilled operator. Fred has learned not to try to take over when minor things go wrong, just as Father

managed to keep out of things all morning. Both
Father and Fred have learned the importance of delegation in their daily work routine.

Is home so different? Is there any reason why Father
cannot apply his knowledge of delegation at home?
More than that, could he not pass on the benefit of his
experience to Mother? She has never been trained to
supervise people, and would probably appreciate some
help along these lines.

Here are some pointers on delegation which Father
might well have taken home along with his vacation
paycheck.

DO'S AND DON'TS OF DELEGATION

DO'S:

1. *Regard Delegation as an Essential Part of Growth
and Development.* Parents should realize that *learning
by doing* is a fundamental rule, and be willing to stand
by while their children make mistakes. Proper delegation can provide the means for children to grow, to
learn to act on their own, and to develop responsibility
and independence. It can also be used to overcome
weaknesses and recognize special abilities. In packing
for Johnny and Susie, Mother lost sight of this, just as
Father did in insisting on loading up the car himself.
Father has been trained not to lose sight of this important principle in his work. Can't he and Mother see
how important it is at home?

2. *Realize the Importance of Delegation as a Means*

of Dividing the Load. Sharing responsibility eases the pressure on the delegator. Both Mother and Father wound up tired and out-of-sorts after a hectic morning of too many minor chores. Father would not have lasted six months without a breakdown on his job as Production Manager if he had not learned to farm out a high percentage of such time- and energy-consuming tasks.

3. *Use Delegation to Encourage Teamwork.* Team effort makes any job more satisfying, and improves both the quality of the work and the morale of those involved. When Mother and Father continually shooed the children away they spoiled half the fun of preparing for the trip, and lost an opportunity to develop closer family ties. And yet this is the same Father who showed his awareness of the advantages of participation when he turned over so much of the installation job to Fred.

4. *Delegate Varying Degrees of Responsibility.* It is important to analyze the situation carefully when you are considering getting a job done through others. The nature of the job should be suitable to the age and ability of the person who is to do it. This is particularly important for parents, since in comparison with adult development, the growth and progress in children are so great and so rapid that continual reassessment of their capabilities is necessary. It is more than likely that in a few weeks or months Susie will be able to cope with the telephone numbers which are beyond her at the moment. Father recognizes at the plant that this is the case with Mac and the other machine operators.

He and Mother would do well to try to recognize it at home.

5. *Define and Establish Standards of Performance and Limits of Responsibility.* Standards should be clearly defined and agreed on in advance. If possible, all concerned should participate in setting them. In business, standards are of primary importance in every job description and in every individual assignment. Fred and Mac know what Father expects of them. Susie and Johnny should have the same advantage.

DON'TS:

1. *Don't Insist on Doing It All Yourself.* We all know how much easier, quicker and more efficient it seems to Do-It-Yourself than to teach someone else to do the job —especially a child. But how are Susie and Johnny ever going to learn to pack suitcases if they are never given a chance to try? Father has taught this principle to Fred; can't he also teach it to Mother? And to himself in his role of parent, as well as Production Manager?

2. *Don't Try to Delegate Everything.* Some things cannot be delegated, such as policy-making and disciplinary powers. Parents and supervisors should learn to distinguish between what is important for them to do personally and what is not. Johnny was all puffed up at being asked to manage Susie, and in slapping her was actually taking over the disciplinary role of his parents. Fred and Mac know that Father makes the final decisions on such matters as safety and discipline, and

that he forms the general policy under which the Finishing Room operates. That's good business management. In fact, it's more than that: it's good common sense.

3. *Don't Regard Delegation as Total Abdication.* The one who delegates is still responsible, for ultimate responsibility cannot be delegated. A follow-up is important for a child who has been given a new task; and with it the assurance of help and co-operation if needed, and of not being punished if the task proves beyond him. It wasn't Susie's fault that she couldn't write down the correct telephone number. Actually, the fault was Mother's. Therefore Mother should not have blamed Susie any more than Father would blame Mac for an error on a job to which he had been assigned without adequate training.

4. *Don't Offer Too Much Help.* Nothing kills initiative faster than the mother-hen brand of supervision. Independence of action is one of the most important elements of growth. Johnny lost all interest in helping with the cat's belongings when his mother checked on his every move. In view of the fact that Father resisted the temptation to hang over Fred's shoulder all Monday morning, why can't he and Mother learn to do the same thing at home?

5. *Don't Forget the Importance of Proper Communication.* Delegation should be firsthand, person-to-person, and take place in a favorable atmosphere. It is no more appropriate or effective for Father to shout directions to Johnny on the run than it would be for him to tell

Fred on his way out to lunch that a new machine has been ordered.

*   *   *

John D. Rockefeller's well-known office maxim states that nobody does anything himself if he can get anybody else to do it. This outlook may have worked out well for Rockefeller, but it can also turn into "passing the buck" or abdication. Formally defined, delegation is the entrustment of responsibility and authority to another person, and the creation of an obligation or accountability for performance. Translating this textbook definition into the terms of family life, we see delegation as the process by which parents allocate to their children appropriate household duties as a means of developing a sense of responsibility.

All of us who have worked in the business world know the supervisor who loosely parcels out all his own work to his subordinates, then sits back, does nothing, and blames them when things go wrong. This is not the delegation we are advocating. A skillful manager uses delegation to get things done through others, while retaining responsibility for the results. In business and industry today's complex problems, both technical and operational, make it imperative for a manager to apply this skill if only to keep his head above water.

Effective delegation is not necessarily second nature to most people. It takes thought and practice. Many management training courses emphasize delegation as a managerial skill, and point out how businessmen can best use it.

There are also convincing reasons why delegation can help in the home as well. First, it is essential to child development. If we wish our children to learn to act on their own, we must make some orderly effort to delegate to them tasks that are within their capabilities or just a little bit beyond. We can help our children to grow by easy stages if we provide a gradual increase in their responsibilities and in each child's obligation for doing his part. One of the first tasks delegated to a young child is that of dressing himself. And what a proud and happy day it is, both for Mother and for Johnny, when at last he manages to struggle into his own sweater! The benefits are mutual, but if fond Mother fails to recognize this fact, and to encourage him to go ahead on his own, she will be tying his shoes until he gets to high school.

Delegation also provides an opportunity for teamwork which can make the most routine family chores more satisfying. Children enjoy working with their parents even in jobs like cleaning up after a meal. The four-year-old is pleased to find that he too can take part by doing some simple task, such as brushing up crumbs or putting out the empty milk bottles. Working together as a team, with each member doing his assigned job, will also improve the quality of the work.

Finally, let us not overlook the advantages to parents of getting the children to take over some of the yard and household chores. Any father who has suddenly discovered that his son can mow the lawn knows how such a division of labor eases the pressure on him as to how

Harry Mace, *American Legion Magazine*

"Look around, get familiar with the place, in a couple of years
you'll be big enough to clean it up."

to allocate his "free" time at home. At first glance this
may seem to be a purely selfish parental view. But a
closer look will reveal that it is an important part of
any general effort toward family harmony. No one en-
joys seeing Mother in the role of martyr as she struggles
through a double load of dishes by herself; nor does
anyone want her to collapse in a tired heap at the end
of the day. Dispositions improve all round if no one
person in the family is overworked. A fair division of
responsibility and of the workload is as vital an aspect
of life in the home as it is in business and in the community.

Most children as they grow up and take their places in the family will find more and more things they like to do—plus some they definitely dislike. For the most part, parents assume that children will automatically take on whatever is expected of them from year to year, just as they proceed from grade to grade in school. This is only partly true. Children will be ready and eager to try some new things, to be sure, but without guidance and instruction they may be reaching in the wrong direction. There are "fun" jobs and unpleasant jobs, varying according to the individual family and child. Which ones can be shared by all the family will depend on the situation, and we will not venture to make suggestions as to who should do which. But parents should be aware of the possibilities—and of the pitfalls—involved in sharing the workload through delegation.

A few words now about some of these pitfalls. It is easy to say: "Delegate, you parents! It's a Utopian family way of life!" But we must quickly add, "Beware!" There are precautions to consider. Once it is decided that a particular job will be delegated, and the plans are discussed by all concerned, it takes a courageous parent to go through with the whole scheme. Your good resolutions may fly out the window when, in looking through it, you see that the lawn appears to have been attacked by a group of amateur barbers instead of the lawnmower. Here is the first warning: Don't rush out to finish the job yourself. Sooner or later the Number One Boy will learn to do a real job—even if it takes all summer. But in the meantime, don't you think he can see the patches he missed? Let *him* repair them.

This standing by amid the chaos of a half-completed task is as difficult for parents as for businessmen. Here is something which requires real self-control: to watch mistakes being made by children or subordinates without batting an eye. But try to remember that anyone learning a new skill is proud of his achievement, and will quickly see ways to improve or correct his performance *if* he is left substantially alone to do so.

Another delegating problem often lost in the shuffle of sudden necessity is posed by the fact that some things should not be delegated at all, despite strong and understandable temptations to the contrary. Parents must retain all disciplinary action and power. Do not allow Junior to punish his little sister for throwing a stone at the neighbor's cat because it is easier than running outdoors to scold her yourself. It is all too simple to suggest that in a parent's absence older children may take on the authority to rule the roost. But unfortunately their ideas of discipline and of the situations calling for it may be poles apart from their parents'. It is important, therefore, to recognize which things can be delegated and which cannot. Most parents realize that they have to retain the power to establish family policy. Bedtimes, rules of health and safety, and the use of the family car cannot be left to immature judgment. These subjects may well be discussed in the family group, but there may need to be some rather potent persuasion to reach an agreement in line with parental thinking.

Next comes the question of how much to delegate. Differences in age and capabilities, plus past experience, must decide; a fifteen-year-old should be allowed more leeway in picking out his clothes, for example, than the younger members of the family. Unusual abilities should be recognized and encouraged; a ten-year-old boy adept at minor electrical repairs might well be allowed to do more of them than his older brother who is more interested in carpentry. Weaknesses in children, such as excessive shyness or lack of mechanical skill, should also be taken into account when parents are delegating. The assigned job can serve as a learning or developmental experience. It should, however, be assigned with a realistic understanding on both parts of what can be expected in the way of results.

Another caution to keep in mind is that no matter how much or how little a parent may delegate to his children, he himself is still responsible for the over-all success or failure of the venture. He cannot pass off the poorly cut lawn as the fault of the boy who is just learning to master the mower. Standards of accountability must be established, so that children have the assurance of being able to proceed in new directions without fear of punishment for mistakes or for total failure. Children will be glad to try new things if they know the parents stand behind them, and if there is no question who is in the main accountable for the family welfare.

The lessons to be learned by allowing children freedom of action within an established sphere cannot be overestimated. We learn by doing; we profit by our mistakes. It all seems so obvious on paper. And yet how many of us have hung over the shoulder of new little cooks with a continuous stream of advice on the progress of the recipe? Leave them alone. Let them leave the eggs out of the waffles this once. If they have to struggle a bit they will learn all the more thoroughly, without losing their eagerness to help.

Even though we may be convinced that the theory of delegation is sound, we may wonder how to go about it in the right way. Below are five pointers to keep in mind when you set out to get Junior to take over the lawn mowing, or any other new job. The whole process of putting these five principles into operation may take only a minute. In some cases, you may even do it without thinking. Or it may take time, thought, and conferring with the others involved. In any case, they are worth keeping in mind.

1. The job at hand, and the situation, must be carefully analyzed to determine what is to be delegated; to whom; when and where; and in what quantity or to what degree. Shall we have our ten-year-old cut the grass this year? Is he able to do it? Is this the kind of job for him or would he be better at taking charge of the pets? What arrangements shall we make with him? How much of the job should he take on? Will he be able to do the trimming and hedge clipping, or should he be responsible only for the mowing? All these questions should be considered by the parents in respect to the boy's strength, health, and aptitudes; to his other

Irving Roir, *American Legion Magazine*

"I hope you remember that tomorrow I'll have been in your employ three years."

commitments at home and outside; and to the responsibilities of the other family members.

2. It is important to establish in advance the standards of performance and the goals we hope to attain. Junior should not be told merely that the lawn is now his job. How much will he be expected to do each week? Under whose direction? May he employ his younger brother to help? What kind of job is passable? Who will help him check on the finished work? What rewards will there be? These questions, too, should be answered at the time the job is delegated, not wrangled over in midstream.

3. No attempt at delegation can even leave the launching pad except in the proper atmosphere, or "favorable climate," as the management jargon would put it. Assurance of help and co-operation if needed must be given by the delegator, and the possibilities of teamwork discussed. If parents and children lack confidence in each other, no delegated project can even start successfully, let alone be carried to a successful finish. Junior will soon get discouraged with the whole idea if he cannot start the power mower and finds that his father has left for a game of golf without explaining its idiosyncrasies.

4. Group spirit, individual challenge or incentive, or some such appropriate motivation, makes up the fourth requirement of effective delegation. Some reason must be provided, or pointed out, for doing the job at hand. Since the reasons are not always apparent, this

aspect of delegation often requires conscious thought
and effort on the part of the parent.

5. Our fifth suggestion may seem too obvious to require mention, but it is nevertheless often overlooked
when we are in a hurry to get something done. This is
the necessity for establishing clear-cut means of communicating amongst all concerned. Discussion of the
job should never be casual or offhand. To be effective,
it should be personal, face-to-face, firsthand. Direct
guidance and counseling should be provided if needed,
just as on-the-job coaching is provided in industry.
Proper communication is essential whether the objective is to teach Susie to beat an egg, or help a stenog-
rapher learn to use a new teletype machine.

We have talked about setting delegation in motion,
but have left until last the equally important subject
of what happens during and after the initial act of delegation. Follow-up and controls are vital parts of the
process. Everything from a casual: "How is it going?"
to a daily or weekly check-up on some long-term family
project should be part of the delegator's job. It does
not make sense to try to encourage a child's development and progress through delegation if, once a task
is assigned, the parent loses interest or appears to forget
all about it. As a matter of fact, most children expect
to give some kind of a progress report, and are eager
to do—sometimes all to frequently!

After the job is started, or even after it is completed,
comes a real chance for development. This is particularly true if the child is encouraged to evaluate the job

himself, through such interested questions from his parents as: "How did you make out pushing the mower around the dogwood tree?," "Did you have any trouble on the front bank?," "What did you learn from today's job?," "Have you any ideas for improving it next time?" By checking over the delegated tasks together, both parent and child can decide how things are going; whether the work is too easy or difficult; how much the child is willing and able to do; and what may reasonably be expected in future accomplishment. Changes in the "ground rules" may be necessary from time to time. Sometimes the child may be trying to do *too* good a job, putting in too much time and effort in proportion to the particular need. Discussion can lead to mutual agreement on all these matters if everyone involved has a chance to speak and be heard.

It should be kept in mind during such evaluations that the expectations of parents and children are likely to differ along the way. Once a job is completed, each is bound to have a different view of the quality of the work and of the degree of completeness. Only by talking it over can understanding be reached, frequently with a certain amount of compromise by the parents. Furthermore, where several children are involved, standards for the same job will vary with age and ability. A fifteen-year-old girl will undoubtedly do a better job of pressing a skirt than her ten-year-old sister. But the ten-year-old may have worked longer and harder, and should not be allowed to get discouraged over the rumpled results. All these factors need consideration when the work of each girl is reviewed and evaluated.

In any follow-up of delegated tasks the most satisfying and effective way to maintain control, to check on the job, and to be sure that all is going well is through the liberal use of praise. Most parents are aware of this fact even though they may never have used some of the other skills mentioned above. Plenty of sincere appreciation for the job under way or just completed contributes a great deal to the success of effective delegation in the home.

VI

Keeping the Family Informed

"SAY, MARG, I almost forgot. Where does this sitter live?" David Munson calls to his wife as he starts out the door.

"Just down at the corner of Broad—number 450. It's Sally Roberts. You'll remember when you see it. I'll try to be ready when you get back."

"Okay. Sally Roberts—number 450.

Nine-year-old Douglas looks up from the television as his mother comes into the living room. "Gee Mom, you look cool. You going out?"

"Yes. We're late now. Have you seen my black purse?"

There is no reply from Douglas. The Bad Guy is hiding behind the door, and Douglas is on the edge of his TV hassock. Five-year-old Sam squeals with alarm as the Good Guy walks into the trap.

"Oh, here it is! We'll be at the Fosters', boys."

Douglas nods, absorbed in the show. Sam is far away in Colorado, completely unaware of his mother's existence.

"Oh, Doug—tell Sally I made up some sandwiches, and I think there's enough ice cream for all of you."

"Ice cream? Hey, neat!" (At last something Mother had to say has penetrated the television curtain.)

The Good Guy's fate is still in doubt when David returns with Sally. "Hi boys!" Sally calls. "How's the show? Hello, Mrs. Munson. My, you look nice."

"Thank you, Sally. I guess I'm all here. It's such a rush to get off at this hour. I fixed you all some sandwiches, and there's ice cream. Just ask Douglas if you have trouble finding anything." (Such as the Fosters' telephone number, Mother?)

"Oh, we'll be all right. Don't worry about a thing. Just have a good time, now."

"Thanks. Let's see—the baby's in bed and the boys will probably be ready to turn in early. They had a big day in the park. Sam's exhausted. Anything else, David?"

David eyes his watch, his mind on the evening ahead. "Guess not. The janitor never turned up to check that bedroom radiator, did he?"

"No. He probably won't come till tomorrow now. What about your Chicago call?"

"I'll try them again in the morning. All set?" He helps her into her coat.

"Yes, thanks. 'Night, boys! Mind what Sally tells you. We shouldn't be very late."

The television gunplay has reached a high point, and even Sally is growing anxious about the outcome. The Munsons' final farewells are drowned out by the Good Guy's .38.

"Whew! I'm glad to get away from that din." Margaret sighs as they head down the hall to the elevator. "We're not *too* late."

In the lobby she stops short. "Oh dear, I forgot to tell Sally about the baby's cough. Should we go back?"

"Oh, no. Doug knows where the cough syrup is if she needs it. She looks as though she could cope. Seems like a nice girl. There's a bus now—let's grab it!" (Guess you'd better—it may be the only one for an hour. And yet . . . ?)

So the Munsons are off for an evening of pleasure, feeling carefree and relaxed with a competent baby sitter in charge. It was hectic getting off, but now everything is under control. (How mistaken can responsible parents be?)

Let's skip over the details of the Munsons' evening, and pick them up again at twelve o'clock. Here they come up the street, sleepy but refreshed by a good dinner and an evening of cards with their friends the Fosters. Margaret looks up as they approach the building. "That's funny. There's a light on in the boys' room."

"Mmmm." David is concerned only with getting the

sitter home as fast as possible and crawling into his warm bed.

The scene which greets them as they open the apartment door is far from the peaceful one they might have imagined. Sally, looking tired and unhappy, is walking the baby, patting him on the back in time to the dance band on television. Lights blaze in every room, and the baby is alternately wailing and coughing.

David hurries to turn off the blaring television as Margaret grabs the baby. "Heavens, Sally, what's the matter? David, get the cough syrup, quick! Has this been going on all evening?"

Sally nods unhappily. "He started around nine, I guess. I tried to call you at the Walters' but there was no answer."

David returns with the cough medicine. "But we were at the *Fosters'*. Didn't you write the number down for her, Margaret?"

"Oh dear, no. But I told Douglas. And didn't he tell you about the cough syrup?"

Sally is close to tears. "No, Mrs. Munson, I'm sorry. He just said you were at the Walters'. He was kind of mad at me anyway when I made him go to bed. He wanted to see the Late Show."

"The Late Show! Good heavens, his bedtime is nine-thirty on weekends. Didn't he tell you? Oh dear, he'll be worn out tomorrow. When *did* he go to bed?"

Sally's reply comes all in a rush. She is a girl with a lot on her mind. "Well, it was pretty late. It was after the janitor came and disconnected the radiator. I didn't know what to tell him was wrong with it, and now there's water all over the boys' floor. As a matter of fact, Douglas was trying to fix it and just quieted down a little while ago."

David rushes down the hall, to find a large puddle on the floor with Douglas asleep on the floor beside it. Sam is in bed, but covered with comic books, some of which have fallen off into the water. He gets Douglas into bed, straightens out Sam, mops up the worst of the water and returns to the living room: Margaret now has the baby calmed down and Sally is standing with her coat on.

"Oh yes, Mr. Munson. Someone called you. It might have been Long Distance. I think the operator gave Douglas a number when he answered, but I was busy with the baby so I'm not sure."

"Oh, good Lord! I tried all afternoon to reach them. Was it from Chicago? Did he write it down? Who was it?"

Sally is thoroughly miserable. "I don't know. I'm sorry. I didn't get it." She makes one final effort: "But anyway, the ice cream was real good, Mrs. Munson."

It appears that the ice cream was the only thing that *was* good at the Munson apartment that evening. In spite of good intentions, the Munsons failed to give Sally the information she needed. Could they have done a better job of preparing her for the evening? David is a businessman. Is he always as casual about his arrangements?

Let us look in on him at his office. David is a salesman, covering a five-state territory for Acme Sales, and
covering it very efficiently indeed. The fact that certain
things have to be done before he embarks on his
monthly swing around the territory is so obvious to him
that he never stops to think about it. After ten years
with Acme, such mechanics have become automatic.

"Here you are, Alice," he says to his secretary. "This
is the itinerary as I see it. Perhaps you'd better write
down the hotels, since I'll be on a different route this
time." He makes sure that the office knows where to
reach him by mail and telephone, and gives Alice a list
of the customers he plans to call on each day.

"What about the quotas from the home office, Mr.
Munson? They're due any day now."

"That's right. You'd better open all the mail and forward the quotas or anything you think might be important. But don't send anything to Joplin after Wednesday or I'll miss it there."

"Are you expecting any calls?"

"Yes. Bill Jones from the Allen Company said he
might call on Tuesday. Maybe Ernie or Norm could
handle him. And on Wednesday old Joe Bryon from
the mill is due to come through. Will you give him the
latest batch of quotations for me? And then on Thurs-
day you'd better make up the monthly expense report
and send it to the usual people."

Alice looks up from her notebook. "Who gets that
expense report now, Mr. Munson? After those last
changes I'm not sure."

David gives her the names, then suggests that she read back his itinerary and the details of the work to be done in his absence. He then checks over his desk calendar to make sure that they have not overlooked anything.

"I'd better add these notes to the calendar in case something comes up while I'm out of the office," Alice suggests. "Here's the money from the cashier, and your plane tickets. You'll notice that you have to change once on the way out, but you can come back nonstop if you catch the three o'clock plane on Friday."

David jots down several details in his own notebook as Alice reviews for him the current status of the various accounts he is to visit on his trip. All in all they have exchanged quite a bit of information in a short time. When David closes his briefcase and reaches for his hat, each one has a clear picture of the events of the coming week. It has been part of David's training as a top salesman for Acme to make sure that everyone in the sales office is kept informed on such matters.

Why the parallel between this situation and the previous one at home did not occur to David is hard to understand. It would not take much time to discuss with Margaret what information they should pass on to the baby sitter, and help her to do so in a businesslike manner. Sally was not very happy as the Munsons' sitter. But perhaps she will be fortunate enough to work in an office with a good boss like David when she gets a little older.

DO'S AND DON'TS OF KEEPING
THE FAMILY INFORMED

DO'S:

1. *Be Sure that the Listener Hears and Understands the Importance of What You Are Saying.* A quick look at Douglas' face would have told his mother that he was too absorbed in television to hear what she was telling him. Even Sally was only half listening when the Munsons left the apartment. It is important for the speaker to make sure that the listener is *attentive*. Parents can help their children learn to pay attention by being good listeners themselves. David has learned this fact at work and would do well to carry it home with him.

2. *Review All Important Points and Ask the Listener to Do the Same.* If Margaret had asked Douglas to repeat back to her the information on where they were going to be for the evening, Sally would have been saved a lot of trouble. The one phrase "ice cream" stuck in Douglas' mind, but not the much more important matter of his parents' destination. David made sure that Alice had all the necessary facts on his business itinerary, but never thought to make a similar check with Sally or Douglas when he left for the evening.

3. *Write Down Important Facts Yourself, or Have the Listener Take Notes.* Whether you make the notes or ask the other person to do so, it is essential to have a written record of telephone numbers and messages, addresses, or other such information. Not only the

Fosters' name and number but also the directions for the janitor and any appropriate information about David's Chicago call and the baby's cough would have helped Sally if they had been written down. David would also have been better off if he and Margaret had taught Douglas to write down all telephone messages when received. This principle is applied as a matter of course in David's office, and would be of equal value in his home.

4. *Ask Questions, Whether Giving or Receiving Information.* "Are you expecting any calls?" would have been as appropriate a question coming from Sally the baby sitter as it was from David's secretary Alice. Since Sally failed to ask for the necessary information, David and Margaret would have done well to ask a few leading questions themselves, such as: "You know how to reach us?" before leaving her with an assortment of problems and inadequate information on how to solve them.

DON'TS:

1. *Don't Rely on Someone Else to Pass On Information For You.* With each exchange, there is less chance of the facts being passed on correctly, particularly where children are involved. The difference between *Foster* and *Walter* did not seem very great to Douglas, but it mattered a good deal to Sally when she tried to reach his parents. It's a wonder they did not rely on five-year-old Sam to tell Sally what she needed to know! All information should be given directly to the person

who is most concerned, as David recognizes in his office when he prepares to go on a trip.

2. *Don't Be Overconfident That You Have All the Information You Need.* When receiving information, take the time to question both yourself and the speaker if you have the slightest doubt about anything he has said or left unsaid. It is important for a parent to master this principle of information-getting himself, and to teach it to his children. Sally was trying to be pleasant and helpful when she said: "Don't worry about a thing," but she would have been a far more efficient baby sitter if she had asked for more complete instructions. Alice was trained to do this in secretarial school, but there is no reason why children cannot learn it at an early age if parents will keep it in mind and try to set a good example.

3. *Don't Try to Give Important Information in a Hurry.* Margaret tried to crowd all the last-minute details into a few sentences when she and David left for the evening, with the result that she omitted some of the most important facts and touched on others too lightly to impress Sally or the boys. David's conversation with Alice was not lengthy, but it was complete. He knew better than to wait until fifteen minutes before plane time to discuss his itinerary with her.

4. *Don't Be Afraid to Interrupt.* Whether you are giving information to someone else or receiving it, it is far better to interrupt the conversation if anything is not clear than to wait until later and risk forgetting your question. When David speaks of "the usual peo-

ple" Alice is not afraid to tell him that she is no longer sure of who they are. If Sally had interrupted the Munsons' exchange of remarks about the radiator and the Chicago call, or questioned Margaret's vague statement about the boys being ready to "turn in early" she would have had an easier evening of baby-sitting.

* * *

One specific application of communication skills is the everyday process of getting and giving information. "They never tell us anything around here" is a familiar protest in the business world. Managers and workers alike have good reason for wanting to know what is going on and how it might affect them. The managements of most firms today are very much concerned with this aspect of employee welfare, for it has been shown that the chances for success in labor relations as well as in production and net income are increased considerably by making a real effort to have an enlightened working force.

Most business concerns are primarily interested in making money, and consequently are willing to invest in anything that improves their financial position. Public relations departments flourish in industrial concerns primarily to keep *employees* informed. Of course they are also concerned with keeping the public informed, but generally share that responsibility with press agents and advertising agencies. Films, employee magazines, letters, bulletin boards, reading racks, as well as the normal flood of office memoranda, use up quite a bit of the customer's dollar—all for a good purpose.

Communication in the opposite direction, from workers to supervisors, can prove more troublesome. Subtler
tactics have to be employed, usually through supervisory education. Even the best of supervisors is bound
to have people working for him who not only fail to
pass on useful information but also operate on the principle of "why should I tell him?" We do not mean to
imply that management has to make informers out of
faithful employees, just that a successful manager will
try to make his workers realize the value of passing on
information that might make for a happier or more efficient work situation.

Military tactics too stress the need for keeping people
informed. Infantry maneuvers are based on maintain-
ing communication in three directions: up, down, and
laterally.

The parallel in the home should be apparent. And
yet few of us think or do very much about it. There is
no earnings statement to be affected, nor any enemy
machine gun to mow us down if we fail to keep our
associates informed. We do not have the time for the
kind of formal information-giving activities mentioned
above. The home movies at our house, although a good
record of family activity in an out-of-focus sort of way,
are intended to entertain rather than to instruct or inform.

With few formal devices at our disposal for keeping
the family informed, we need to look at some general
principles and skills. Actually, when we consider these
principles and skills we are struck by their simplicity.

There are no magic formulas. But there is much to be
gained just by organizing our thoughts. Awareness and
practice are what count in human relations, not book
knowledge alone.

Children frequently try to give us information, but
find us too busy to be bothered, or for some reason unable to get the message. This inability to "get through"
is something we condemn in our children but seldom
think of as applying to ourselves. If you really want to get
information and get at the truth, you must give full
attention and show interest when your children talk to
you. Try to assure them that you realize the importance
of what they are saying.

When a child dashes into your bedroom at six o'clock
in the morning, he may not only be seeking a ready
adult ear but also some assurance of action if necessary.
Even though his idea of action may be quite different
from your own at that hour, at least you can indicate
readiness to defend his cause or mend the wrong. Be
appreciative when your children do tell you things. By
encouraging them to talk freely, you may have to listen
to a lot that is not at all important or interesting, but
this is surely much better than closing the communication gate entirely.

The general principles of the last two paragraphs
should also apply when you wish to give information to
children. They too must be made aware of the necessity
of being attentive and of understanding that you have
something of value to pass on. We all know how
frustrating it can be to make a suggestion which is

greeted with a dull stare or a negative shake of the head.

There is a children's game which emphasizes what can happen to information as it is passed from one person to the next. Seated around a table, one person starts by whispering a word or a short sentence into the ear of the person on his right. The message is passed from one to the next to see what comes out when it has gone all around the table. The end result, which rarely resembles the starting phrase, provides great amusement. This same sort of change in the nature of information happens to us all the time, with results which are not always funny. Neighborhood rumors, the well-known office grapevine, and the children's tall tales of what they heard at school are all subject to various types of change along the way.

There are several techniques which can be used to

MORTY MEEKLE   Nice Try, Winthrop!

prevent loss of information when you are talking with
your children. Their use will depend on the formality
of the situation and the type of exchange taking place.
In an office, most people would hate to be caught without a pad and pencil when they are given news of the
latest salary changes. When old enough to write, children will enjoy taking notes about things you tell them
if you encourage such a procedure. We all know how
quickly they forget such verbal messages as when the
next choir practice will be held, or where you said you
would be waiting for them after school.

When you are trying to pass on a great many details,
try to keep them in logical order. Once you have presented your story be sure to go back over the most important things. It may be helpful to have the children
give you an idea of what they have understood from

Dick Cavalli, reproduced by permission of NEA Service, Inc.

you, so long as this is not merely repeating your words by rote.

Try to get your children to slow down and think of what they are saying as they relay their reports on the day's doings. You will do well to remember this when you are doing the talking. No matter how well organized you are ahead of time, once under way you may speak too rapidly or enumerate too many things for young minds to grasp. Whenever possible, use emphasis to clarify an important point. By this we do not mean shouting or threatening. But try to stress the important words. The only things that Junior really needs to remember from a discussion of an overdue library book are "book," "today," and *"ten-cent fine."*

Using maps, calendars, pictures, or other visual materials may help in some types of information giving. Reference to the calendar or clock will help reinforce through the eye what the ear has been hearing. Encouraging children to draw maps and sketches will help them describe things to you, and serve also to develop artistic skill.

Sometimes we are so anxious to put across an idea to the children that we unconsciously discourage them from talking. They may want to listen, and be showing keen attention, but still be afraid to interrupt for fear of being reprimanded or of sounding stupid in front of the others. It may be helpful for you to ask: "What would you like me to go over again?" or "What questions does this bring up?" This should be done not only at the end of the discussion, when a review or summary is in order, but during the conversation as well, so that nothing will get lost along the way.

So many things can happen during an exchange of information that it is hard to know which type of change is the worst. Additions, embellishments, and fabrications are particularly common among young children, whose imaginations are just too active not to embroider. No matter who is involved, inaccuracies are likely to result as information goes from person to person. An experiment not unlike the children's game mentioned above is used in some business classrooms to demonstrate the problems involved in passing on information. Observers record what is said as a story is relayed from one to another in a group of five or six persons. It usually develops that there is a loss of information which follows a definite pattern, with over fifty per cent lost in the first conversation, the loss continuing to a point where only ten to twenty per cent of the original facts are relayed to the last person. Additions and changes may occur, too, but the loss is the most noticeable. If this is a typical adult pattern, what can we expect from our children?

Personality differences enter into the problem of oral relay of information. The positive child may interpret a tentative statement as a definite fact, whereas the shy child may do just the opposite, passing on what he has been told in a vague and uncertain manner.

There are several specific situations which come up regularly in business and in the home which illustrate the need for keeping others informed. In business, new policies and practices are introduced with care and attention. The same principle should apply at home. When parents agree on a new plan for paying allowances or keeping the cellar tidy, they should apply the above-mentioned techniques of information, and give the new plan more than just a casual mention. If you are in business, you know that changes in schedules or deadlines receive a great deal of attention. But how well do you do at home in discussing new bedtimes, or letting the children know in advance that you plan to usurp the television set for the football game during their daily cartoon show?

It is important to tell the whole family of an impending trip or visit from Aunt Mabel just as soon as plans are final. Like the office worker, who prefers to get the official word rather than pick up rumors via the grapevine, your child should have the advantage of straightforward, prompt dissemination of family news from the one source he believes unimpeachable, instead of overhearing it through conversational snatches which are easily misinterpreted by his imaginative young mind.

Children cannot be expected to take on the full responsibility of keeping the family informed, but we should encourage them to try. Parents can set a good example by bringing home pertinent news of the neighborhood, town and world. Intelligent discussion at home of everything from local taxes and plans for a new school to politics and foreign policy will help the children to realize what is going on around them, and will stimulate them to ask questions and learn more about life in general. The silent father preoccupied with his television show offers his children little opportunity to satisfy their great and natural curiosity. Whether the news is of the family or of the outside world, it should be exchanged in a clear and understandable manner in order to keep the home running smoothly and to avoid communication chaos.

VII

Holding Family Conferences

HERE IS A PEACEFUL SCENE. Ben Sr. is the only one at home in the Miller household, and he could not possibly be more comfortable. Feet up, pipe in hand, a bowl of apples at his side, and the West Coast football championship play-off on television: master of all he surveys, his only worry whether or not California will block that kick. His wife Blanche has gone to market, and the boys are in the midst of an exciting acorn war, their shouts just far enough away to be reassuring but not intrusive. Who could ask for anything more?

It is all very well except that it cannot last. The kick is blocked; the announcer interrupts for station identification—it must be five-thirty. Ben stretches comfortably and is urged by a friendly face on the screen to get himself a beer. The spell is broken by a slamming door and excited voices. These include not only those of his

own two boys but also their three best friends, still
arguing about the last battle but ready to settle their
differences in front of the television, while cheering on
their common cowboy hero.

"I get the TV hassock!"

"You do not. It's my turn!"

Ben Jr. is in the lead as the Miller boys catch sight
of their father. "Hey, Dad, it's five-thirty. Okay to
switch channels?"

"Sorry, boys, I'm watching the football game." (Ben
as yet has no realization that This Is It.)

"But it's time for the Texas Kid! We always watch
it. Football games are over at five-thirty."

"Not this football game, Junior. I told you this was
on the West Coast."

Ben Jr. is almost too indignant to speak—but not
quite. "This is the Texas Kid on *Granite Mountain!*
Channel 3." As leader of the outfit, he takes matters in
hand and switches the knob. (At last Ben Sr. begins to
realize that he has Real Trouble.)

The back door slams and Blanche calls a cheerful
greeting. Lamb chops were surprisingly cheap because
of the late hour, and she is feeling happy and trium-
phant. She has even forgiven Ben and his football game
for usurping her regular afternoon quiz show. "Hello,
everybody! I'm home!" she calls again. "Someone want
to give me a hand with these groceries?"

But no one hears. The lines are now drawn in the
living room.

"I tell you I'm watching the footfall game on Channel 8. You boys will just have to give up your program this once."

"But we *can't*. We hafta see it this week. The Texas Kid's in real trouble, I told you. It's much more important than an old football game."

"Now listen here, this is a championship game and I'm watching it and this is my house! You boys stop making a fuss and go watch it somewhere else if it's so important." Ben rises angrily to turn the knob back again to Channel 8.

"We can't! It's already started. Mommmeee! Dad won't let us watch our show!" Ben Jr. is furious; his younger brother in tears; the neighbors silent and wary, ready to egg on their champion whenever they can, but a little afraid of Mr. Miller's rising temper.

Blanche comes in from the kitchen, prepared to mediate. "What seems to be the trouble?"

Ben Jr., Mark, and their companions all join in to tell her exactly what seems to be the trouble.

"Dad's had the TV all afternoon, and now he won't let us watch the Texas Kid!"

"Gee whiz, it's not fair."

Two or three more echoes: "No, it's not fair!"

"For Pete's sake, Blanche, can't you straighten these kids out? I'm watching the game and they're getting out of hand about their silly show. It's time they learned who's boss around here." (Is this the ideal moment to teach them, Dad?)

Blanche's good mood vanishes. She recalls that this was the afternoon a new challenger was to appear on *her* show. "Yes, I *know* you're watching the game. Come, boys, let's not disturb Mr. Miller any more now. He's too busy with important matters. I'll make you all some popcorn, and you two can watch TV an hour later tonight to make up for missing this one. None of us must disturb the Boss!"

The boys are mollified by these unusually generous offers, but the day is spoiled for both Ben and Blanche. The lamb chops will be consumed in hurt silence, judging by the acid in Blanche's tone, and Ben will have to do better than make popcorn to win any friends around the house or neighborhood for the next few days. *And all over a silly television program. Why can't his family act like human beings over a little thing like that?*

If Ben Miller would consult one of the members of his car pool, he might get some tips on how to make his family act like human beings, even over television. George Becker works for the same firm that Ben does, and lives just a block away. They were both called into company headquarters last spring for a course on conference leadership. The Beckers have a more complicated household than the Millers. It includes George and his wife Marion, their teen-age daughter Ann, twin eight-year-old boys, a baby girl, and Marion's father, who lives with them six months of the year. The one television set in their living room used to be the source of many arguments, until it occurred to George to put the conference method to work on Dogwood Drive. Here is how it works at his house:

The Becker family knows that on the evening George comes home with the weekly television guide, their regular TV conference is in order. Just to make sure, Marion reminds them all at supper time to meet in the living room at eight o'clock. Marion brings the family engagement calendar and George produces the guide. Grandfather and the children are given a chance to look it over before the meeting starts.

George usually acts as leader and moderator, bringing into his home all the skills he learned at the company course. He may open the discussion by reminding everyone that although the television schedule is the main topic, this is also a good time to bring up any other relevant matters, such as problems of scheduling rides, homework, or extracurricular activities for the coming week. Ann has asked him to bring up the slumber party she would like to hold next Friday. Does Mother have any objections? Do the boys have any conflicting requests? Does Grandpa mind giving up his room just this once? Now is the time to bring up any questions or suggestions. George has jotted down a few other notes before launching into the main discussion. Are there any additions?

If not, where is the television guide? Make sure that it is handy, so that no one's favorite program will be overlooked. It is Ann's turn to be secretary—is she all set to take notes? George employs all his best conference-leading methods and techniques as they discuss the week's program. Each member of the family speaks up for the shows he is most interested in. They all have learned that in this forum they will receive a much more impartial hearing than if they try to shout their wishes over the noise of the television program they hope to supplant.

As he was taught to do, George listens carefully to all ideas, occasionally stepping in to get the discussion back on the track or urge that the argumentative twins pause long enough to let Grandpa be heard. Mother's favorite opera; Grandfather's old-time movie; sister Ann's dance band; and the twins' Western serials all come up for review, plus any special features of the week. Sometimes it takes a bit of juggling. If their parents are going to be out on Saturday night, may the children watch Uncle Peter's Playhouse? May the twins stay up an hour later than usual to see the opening night of the circus? Since Ann's midyear exams start Monday, she will have to go to bed before her regular quiz show. Perhaps Grandpa would enjoy seeing the fight that night for a change?

Occasionally there is no way to resolve a conflict except to take a vote. The twins have learned to get together on this if on nothing else. George winds up the conference by asking for questions, having Ann read back the schedule as it is now worked out, and making sure that everyone agrees. Any other topics which have been suggested are handled in the same manner, and the Becker family is ready for the week's activities, television and otherwise, with a minimum of arguing. Thanks to their weekly conference, they manage to stay friends in spite of television.

DO'S AND DON'TS OF HOLDING
CONFERENCES

DO'S:

1. *Hold a Conference to Plan Family Activities and Policies.* Both regularly scheduled meetings and those called for a special purpose can be a real help to better understanding within the family. Such meetings make it possible for everyone to get a fair hearing, and to air their views and grievances. They also provide an opportunity to settle family questions in a friendly way, as George Becker learned when he brought home what he had learned at work about conference leadership. Through participation in family meetings you can teach, train and develop your children. They can learn from you how to disagree without losing friends or holding grudges, and, best of all, can learn not to "go away mad."

2. *Plan and Prepare in Advance for All Conferences.* Be sure of the main purpose of the meeting, and that all who will be present know just what it is. If you are in charge, plan a convenient time and place and let everyone know about it ahead of time. Prepare the agenda, also in advance if possible. As leader, have some kind of guide in the form of mental or written notes, and see that any necessary equipment is available. The fact that the Becker family was well prepared, with comfortable surroundings and the necessary television guide and calendar, contributed to the success of their conference.

3. *Encourage Active Participation From Everyone Who Is Present.* Use leading questions to encourage participation, and be sure to give genuine consideration to all opinions. Giving the children their chance to speak is of no value unless they feel that some attention is being paid to what they have to say. After a thorough discussion, the leader should guide the group to evaluate the results. A vote may be the most appropriate means to insure that all take part in the decision as well as the discussion. Participation by all leads to better understanding and sounder decisions, and children learn more about making their own decisions if they have a chance to contribute in such a way at home. All members of George Becker's family took part in the television conference except the baby—when she learns to talk she will be urged to participate too!

4. *Listen Actively and Speak Clearly, as Leader or Participant.* Children must learn to keep alert and to listen to the opinions of others whether they want to or not. They can also learn from your example to use facts and concrete examples as a means of strengthening their case and making their points understandable. Through holding regular family conferences as the Becker family does, this valuable training is easily absorbed; whereas no one listened to anyone else during the free-for-all over television in the Miller household which resulted in antagonism and hurt feelings.

DON'TS:

1. *Don't Try to Settle Important Family Matters Without Consulting Every Member.* It is difficult to settle anything by consulting one person at a time in a haphazard way. The Beckers have learned that it is much easier and more effective to get everyone together and get a consensus whether the problem is unusual or routine. As we saw in the Miller household, a last-minute rearrangement of the television schedule may lead to quarrels and bad feeling if there has been no advance consultation.

2. *Don't Dominate a Conference by Being an Autocratic Leader.* As leader, would-be leader, or willing participant, try to be aware of the whole group instead of being self-centered. If a conference is to be successful, each member must listen to the opinions of others and keep his own mind open. The leader in particular must restrain his urge to jump into the conversation. This is particularly hard when children are involved, but vitally important, as George Becker and his family have learned, both through his training in conference leadership and through their own experience with regular family conferences at home.

3. *Don't Be Afraid to Voice Your Opinions or to Ask Questions.* Whether you are the leader or the newest member of the group, do not hold back for fear of being laughed at or talked down. If you have a tolerant, co-operative attitude toward the opinions of others, they will usually reciprocate. Even the ideally dem-

Drawing by Steig, © The New Yorker Magazine, Inc.

"B-plus is not good enough for a Zimmerman!"

ocratic leader has a right to state his feelings and opinions, as long as he does not force them on the group. By example, parents can show their children that even the silliest-sounding suggestions may have some merit and deserve consideration if they are offered in a sincere manner. Three generations take part in the Becker family meetings, and each member has learned to "speak up in meeting" thanks to George's encouraging attitude, and the interest shown by the others.

4. *Don't Let a Conference Dissolve Into an Aimless Discussion.* It is important for the parent or leader to keep the meeting moving in the right direction, if he can do so in a democratic way. Even the most informal session should be prevented from going too far afield to be of value. The leader must guide and control the discussion and keep it to the point. In so doing, he should summarize, interpret if necessary, and analyze frequently what the others have said. He must keep the purpose in mind at all times, and urge the other members to do the same. And difficult as it is when children are among the participants, he should try to shut off the chatterboxes and the ones who enjoy bickering, as George has learned to do with his twin sons.

* * *

Figures available on the percentage of time spent in conferences by the average businessman show that such meetings play a most important part in the whole communications system. It is also evident that employee participation in making decisions and forming policy results in high morale and efficient job performance.

In the home, just as in business, in the community, and in our government, one-man rule is on the wane. It may be amusing to read about the days of *Life With Father,* but we recognize that this is a period picture, no longer reflecting the life of a typical American household. In the home as in business, participation by all members of the family—or at least by all those who can talk—in meetings and conferences leads to better understanding and sounder decisions on policy making and problem solving.

Another notable change is seen in methods of handling children at school. The degree of freedom of action allowed schoolchildren is so much greater than that of Father's day that only conflict can result in the family which resists this increasing latitude through the use of autocratic rule at home.

There are several types of meetings and conferences in business which can be used at home in an informal way. In a business corporation, major policy decisions are often reached through the regular staff meeting. Department chiefs, advisors, and operating heads usually participate in a staff meeting, and while the top-ranking man present may run the *meeting,* still the entire group runs the *business.*

At home the staff meeting in the form of a regular family get-together can also be of value. In some circumstances, it may be just the two parents who sit down after church on Sunday to talk about immediate plans or long-range projects for the family; clothing to buy; the bank account that needs balancing; or any other question of this nature. Better still, the whole family may take part in a conference to discuss the weekend plans, to decide what chores need to be done, and to agree on who will do them. Policies as to the use of the back-yard sandbox, the family car or television may be worked out; or Father may use the time to help the boys with their knot tying or carpentry projects.

At first glance, the regularly scheduled staff meeting may seem too formal for family use, but it need not be. One advantage it has over haphazard meetings is that the children know that they will have an opportunity to present their ideas and get a democratic hearing. They will look forward to the chance to talk with their parents about camping trips or museum expeditions, and eventually realize that this is a better way to put their ideas across than by shouting them to Mother while she is hanging out the weekly wash.

Just as in business situations, there are also times when family meetings have to be called for special reasons. Such meetings do not necessarily involve the whole family every time. How many people take part will depend on the nature of the problem or situation under discussion, but the main difference between family conferences and the interviews which we discussed in Chapter II is that usually more than two people are involved.

The special meeting or conference may also involve relatives, friends, or neighbors. (For our purposes it makes no difference whether the last two are synonymous.) Neighborhood disputes may be settled at such meetings, and agreement reached on rules. Schedules for driving the boys on the block to scout meetings or baseball practice can best be worked out by the whole group involved, including the children.

Consider holding a conference when you have to establish unpopular rules for your children and their friends. It may help you in telling them that they cannot fly kites from the roof; that they are not to run through Mrs. Kelly's flower garden; or that there must be no ball playing in front of the picture window. If such rules are discussed in the presence of other children and parents, many questions and conflicts can be avoided. Your own children will realize that they are not the only ones subjected to harsh regulations. If all the children and parents involved can talk together about the problems and dangers of stringing wires across the street for a telegraph set, the budding inventor will be less able to put pressure on a reluctant father, and may even be persuaded to try his Morse code with mirrors instead.

We are not concerned in this book with meetings and committee or club work outside the home, but we do want to point out that many of the principles set forth are applicable and worth consideration by parents who are involved in community activities.

All conferences require some advance planning. Such preparations as advance notice to participants, a clearly stated purpose and agenda, and detailed outlines of new policies or practices contribute a great deal to the success of a business conference. The same principle applies at home whenever a meeting seems to be the best solution to a particular problem, or at the regular weekly meeting time. Be sure that all who will attend know just what you have planned. It may be better to cancel the weekly meeting if there is nothing worth talking about. Let the children know that you plan to discuss a summer work schedule, or tell the neighbors that a new scout committee for your district is being formed. Sometimes it is helpful to take the time to write out your own ideas of the purpose of the meeting.

Within the family the personalities of the group are well known, and behavior can be predicted fairly accurately. But if the neighbors are involved, it may be worth while to make an effort to analyze the people who will take part in the conference. Make a mental note that John Schmidt never opens his mouth if he can help it, and be prepared to deal with that argumentative Mr. Wilson next door. Others may be overly talkative, obstinate, or complaining. One of your advance tasks should be to figure out how to handle each one if he causes his own brand of trouble.

Planning what topics are to be covered is an important part of preparing for a conference. The people who are to meet should participate in this if possible. The agenda for a formal conference may be written down and distributed. Where the family group alone is concerned, this is probably unnecessary, as long as one parent has a definite idea of what is to be discussed. An outline or leader's guide, in the form of written or

mental notes, will help insure that no part of the agenda
is forgotten once the meeting is under way.

Other advance preparations for meetings should include adequate notice to all concerned of the time and
place; choosing an appropriate location for the meeting
where comfortable surroundings are assured; and pro-
viding any necessary equipment such as paper, pencils,
and calendar.

Conference leadership is the concern of many adult
self-development courses. This is a big subject, particularly for the business manager whose skill in it
may lead to a successful career. Observation of the democratic process is the most important single principle of
leadership which he must learn. The amount of participation by the group will depend on the attitude of
the leader. A conference dominated by an autocratic
leader will not leave anyone happy or satisfied with
what is accomplished.

When the chief purpose of the meeting is to instruct
or inform, the parent or leader may have to talk quite
a bit. But whenever problems are to be solved, or decisions made, the leader should encourage participation
and restrain his own urge to jump into the conversation
every time he sees an opening. Children should be
urged to contribute, and their ideas should be given
real consideration. When there is a difference of opinion, taking a vote may be the only way in which the
matter can be settled amicably.

Through a family conference, such matters as picking a name for a new pet can become a group decision,

acceptable to all, instead of the object of bickering and strife. The technique known as "brainstorming," a type of group creativity which has been tried in business to produce new ideas, can be applied in modified form in the home. Whether group creativity is superior to that of individuals is open to question in the world of science and business, but we know that children will gleefully spur one another on to imaginative heights with a slight amount of direction and control from a parent or leader. In the brainstorming process anything goes at first—the crazier the suggestions for the new dog's name the better. The leader should write them all down, and encourage the children to think of as many names as possible, and not to hold back for fear of ridicule. They will enjoy this, probably to the point of silliness at times, but might very well be expected to produce forty or fifty names in a short time. The next step is to go back over the list to see whether still more names are suggested by those already written down. The leader's main responsibility is to encourage each child to contribute at least one or two names, and to make general suggestions as to the type of name they may want to consider. He should have them narrow the list down, and consider voting for the final selection. Generally the solution will be a happy one because the children have been allowed free play of the imagination, in which they delight and excel.

A brief gathering of the family clan may be helpful prior to the arrival of guests. Even if the occasion is a simple one, such as the grandparents' coming out for dinner, it may be well to make sure that everyone knows about it and is appropriately scrubbed and polished. If the visit is for a weekend, a longer conference may be needed to discuss sleeping and eating arrangements, schedule changes, and any special habits, likes, or idiosyncrasies of the visitors.

Whether a conference is simple or complex, the parent as leader should give some thought to the leadership skills emphasized in business. He must start and guide the discussion, and make sure that all take part. He should not appear to be self-centered, but may present his views for group consideration just as he encourages the children to do. Most important, he must *listen*. He should keep the purpose of the meeting in mind at all times, and not let it deteriorate into aimless prattle or inappropriate complaint. It is difficult enough in a meeting of adults for the leader to keep from dominating the discussion, but when children are involved, it may seem almost impossible. But the fact remains that it is the leader's behavior that determines whether or not the group reaches a true democratic decision.

Let us run through some of the mechanics of leading a conference which are automatically applied in business. At first these techniques may seem too formal for use in the family or neighborhood meeting, but we believe that many of them will prove helpful even in the simplest situation, and that a businesslike approach will be of value no matter what the occasion.

When all members of the group have gathered, first put them at ease, remind them of the purpose of the meeting, and briefly review the topic to be discussed. Appoint one of the children to act as secretary and take notes. The leader may then present the facts, his opinions if appropriate, and some general or specific questions for the group to answer, as a means of encouraging everyone to participate. If necessary, he may introduce visual aids to help the discussion.

From this point on, the parent or leader should more or less sit back and let the others talk. He may have to repeat statements of others to be sure that they are cor-

Drawing by George Price, © 1959 The New Yorker Magazine, Inc.

"A copy of Robert's 'Rules of Order.'"

rectly understood by all, or summarize youthful ramblings. He may wish to ask questions or opinions of the silent members, or shut off the more loquacious ones. It may also be necessary when children are present not only to guide the discussion and keep it under control, but also to act as a mediator and policeman if any physical violence breaks out, as we have seen happen in our family.

When it appears that all relevant opinions and facts have been stated, it is up to the leader to guide the group to evaluate them. Try to have the children work out a consensus or a solution. After an agreement is reached on what is to be done, discuss any action that may be necessary, or simply close the meeting.

A parent can also set a good example as a participant in the conference whenever he or she is not acting as the leader. You may have recognized that leading the meeting requires tact and skill, without thinking about the responsibilities of participation. Anyone who has led meetings will agree that the attitude and manner of the people attending is what makes things easy or difficult. Co-operation, tolerance of other people's opinions, awareness of the group, open-mindedness, and tact are all important. Children find it particularly hard to learn how to listen to the opinions of others, and it is even more difficult for them to compromise or yield completely than it is for their elders. They must be shown that they can disagree without being tactless or unpleasant; and they must learn to accept cheerfully the decision of the group even when they do not agree with it.

In addition to listening actively and remaining alert, they should be encouraged by your example to speak distinctly and stick to the point in hand. Show them how to use facts and examples, to give sincere opinions, and to make their points in an understandable way. Parents should be alert to all of the opportunities provided by the family conference. A child can be made to accept a suggestion more readily when carried along by the group spirit than if the same suggestion is made to him alone. Some of the above procedures may seem farfetched when applied to a meeting of six- and eight-year-old children, but informal "buzz sessions" and even formal meetings can be considered developmental tools for children, just as the leadership of conferences has become one of the chief skills of management development in industry. Try a formal conference to make plans for your next family weekend trip, keeping the above fundamentals in mind. The results may come as a pleasant surprise.

VIII

Planning for the Family

NOT LONG AGO Louise and Carl Gilbert read an article which described the joys and advantages of starting a garden as a family project. Now, having just moved into their new home, with the back yard not yet seeded, they see an ideal opportunity. "It's something we can all do together this year," they agree. "It will give the children a chance to learn to work as a group."

On the first sunny Saturday, Carl dashes off to the hardware store, full of spring fever and enthusiasm. Returning home, he breaks the good news to his family. "Say, everybody, come see what I got uptown—seeds for our garden!"

His four children, ranging in age from five to twelve, cluster around him to see the seed packets. Nine-year-old Chic makes the first grab. "Can I have the radishes? I love radishes!"

"Me too," chimes in younger brother Bill. "Can I have some too?"

"Where are the flowers?"

"Oooh, corn! Lemme have the corn."

"Stop it, Kenny! I had it first."

The rising voices bring Louise in from the porch.

"Now, now, everybody. This a *family* garden. Let's take the seeds outdoors and see where they'll all go. It's a perfect day to start the garden."

"But where are the flowers?" Peggy insists. The eldest child and only girl in the family, Peggy has a mind of her own.

"Sorry, Peg, no flowers. There won't be room if we want to grow all these vegetables."

"Gee, some garden!" grumbles Peggy. "I hate vegetables." With no further interest in the "family" garden, she returns to her mystery story. (First casualty. Too bad Carl closed his mind to the possibility of a few flowers.)

Carl and Louise and the three boys file out into the back yard to survey the terrain. "Now let's see—this flat strip across the back is the best place, I guess. You boys run and get the tools and we'll get right at it."

But the boys are busy forming their own plans for the garden, each with a slightly different idea.

"Where do the peas go?"

"How about a rock garden?"

"Can I plant the corn? Where's the corn?"

"Kenny has all the seeds. Hey, Kenny, gimme the peas!"

Five-year-old Kenny refuses angrily. "They're *my* peas. Where's *my* garden?" (None of this is quite what Carl had in mind.)

"Let's not argue, boys. We're nowhere near ready for the seeds. First we have to get the ground ready. We'll need the hoe, and the spade, and both rakes. You boys go find them while I measure it off here."

Bill and Chic manage to dig up the spade and one rake. Kenny returns, clutching a small trowel, and dragging the snow shovel. As the older two begin to argue over the rake, Louise steps in, trying hard to get things organized. "Wait a minute, boys. Let's figure out how we're going to work it. Shall we divide up the space so that each one takes care of his own plants?" (Nice try, but not in keeping with Carl's idea at all.)

"No, no, we'll all share the work just as we share the vegetables. That's the real family way—just one big garden for everyone." Unaware of this philosophy, Kenny is now digging away in a far corner with his trowel, humming to himself, "My garden is the best garden 'cause it's *my* garden."

Chic and Bill raise their usual objections: "But I want just radishes."

"I want radishes too, and I want corn."

"No, boys, that is *not* the way to go about it. We'll start with the peas, because they're the earliest. Let's see—early peas—mid to late March. Hmmm—guess we

should have had them in a few weeks ago at that."
(First realization that this might have been planned
better, Carl?)

"Never mind, we'll just have them a little late this
year. They'll still be good." With this, Louise returns
to the house, feeling that she has contributed all that
she can at this stage.

"It says that the corn should be planted in hills three
feet apart," Chic offers. "Will we have enough room,
Dad?"

"Not quite enough, I guess. Maybe we'd better skip
the corn this year." (The crows would probably eat it
anyway.)

"Gee whiz, we gotta have corn! I love corn."

"Now look here, boys, we won't have anything if we
don't get going here. I'll turn over the soil and you can
all follow me with the rakes." Chic and Bill resume
their running argument over the lone rake. Bill loses
out and goes off angry, leaving Carl and Chic to put
in an hour of hard work, punctuated by a few unsuc-
cessful attempts to get Bill back and to get Kenny to
join in. Exhausted by the unaccustomed exercise, Carl
retreats to the house to rest up a bit, calling again to
Bill to help Chic with the lumps and stones.

On his return he finds the back yard deserted except
for Kenny, who is happily pouring out all of the seed
packets into neat holes in his small garden. By this time
Carl is both lame and discouraged. He concludes that
the whole garden idea is hopeless, that his family is
too disorganized for such a project. This was not at all

the way the article described it. *What's the matter with this family, anyway?*

Perhaps the most puzzling aspect of the failure of the Gilberts to start a family vegetable garden is the fact that Carl himself put so little thought into how to launch such a project. It hardly seems necessary to protest that he really knows how to plan a venture when we find that as manager of the local office of a large insurance company, he is supervisor of twelve salesmen and a clerical staff of thirty-five girls. Planning ahead, assembling and organizing his resources to carry through his plans, and checking up to make sure that they are being carried through effectively, is such a fundamental part of this job that he never has to think about it.

Carl's planning responsibilities include everything from the long-range goal of establishing quotas for his sales force for the coming year to such immediate objectives as getting everything ready for the regular monthly visit from the district manager, or simply finding enough time to eat lunch during a busy day of appointments and conferences.

Let us look over Carl's shoulder as he prepares to greet the district manager, Harold Craig. He assembles all the sales reports they will need to go over together; his figures on expenses and the hours each person on the staff has put in during the past month; the charts prepared by headquarters on the predicted sales over a six-month period; and finally his notes on the new data-processing machine he has asked to have installed this spring.

When Carl and Harold sit down to go over the monthly reports they may have several objectives in mind. The content of the reports is not news to either of them, but they both know the value of analyzing the figures together. Perhaps there is a problem concerning the work force. The graphs show that a five per cent increase in the number of accounts over last year is anticipated. Can the present staff handle this increase? Or should another girl be hired? Will there be any personnel losses during the next few months as far as anyone knows? How many hours have been allocated to train the girls who will use the new machine? And to what extent will the machine increase the hourly output? After careful analysis of present and future needs, Carl and Harold make plans to hire one additional girl.

Next they may proceed to a discussion of the new machine. Where will it be located? Will it crowd the girls at that end of the office? They go over the various alternatives in the light of the most efficient use of existing space and of convenience to all the girls concerned. By the time their interview is over, Carl and Harold may have touched on half a dozen more topics, large and small, all related to their mutual interest in the business. Both men have been trained to plan ahead and to organize their time, personnel, and physical resources effectively as a means of running an efficient and productive insurance office. The Gilberts' garden would have been off to a better start if Carl had thought to bring some of this training home with him for back-yard application.

PLANNING DO'S AND DON'TS

DO'S:

1. *Plan Your Course of Action in Advance.* When Carl Gilbert impulsively dashed off to the hardware store without consulting the rest of his family, he went counter to all he had learned at work about planning and organizing. The children were bound to wrangle about seeds and tools if no advance thought was given to what each one wanted, and what each was to do. At the office, Carl looks several months ahead on matters of personnel and equipment. Surely the summer-long garden project merited at least a half-hour conference, and a brief review of the garden books.

2. *Keep Your Plans Simple and Flexible.* One reason why the garden project failed was that Carl was unwilling to change the vague and ambitious plan he had in his own mind. Peggy's interest could have been held by adding a few pansies; Kenny would have been happy with one packet of seeds and a corner all his own; Louise and the other two boys had an idea or two to contribute if given half a chance. At his desk, Carl gives consideration to other people's ideas and suggestions, whether they come from the district manager or the office boy. Why not show the same flexibility at home?

3. *Use an Analytical Approach to Planning.* Because

Carl did not stop to analyze in advance what would be needed to get a garden off to a good start, he was unable to see what caused his project to fail. He would have done better to sit down with his family and determine their needs and wants as well as the methods for carrying them out, just as he did with Harold Craig at the office. From eight to five, Monday through Friday, Carl gathers facts, analyzes alternatives, decides on a plan, and arranges to carry it out. Why not apply the same methods on Saturday?

DON'TS:

1. *Don't Launch a Project Without Checking All Your Resources.* At the insurance office, Carl and his district manager considered personnel, methods, space, equipment, and time when they laid their plans for the months to come. It is all too obvious that Carl did not think of any of these important factors when he planned a garden that was a) started too late for peas; b) too small for corn; and c) prepared by members of his family whose degrees of interest varied and who were inadequately equipped with tools.

2. *Don't Abandon a Good Idea Because of the Lack of an Over-all Plan.* Basically, the Gilberts' idea of a family garden was an excellent one. But because it was not planned and organized in advance, all the minor things that went wrong combined to make it fail. An over-all plan which spelled out each person's responsibilities, the time sequence, and the methods to be

used would have saved the project, spared Carl's disappointment, and kept the family in vegetables.

3. *Don't Overlook the Importance of a Follow-up.* Be sure to check to see that the results conform as nearly as possible to the original plan. Carl could hardly expect his boys to finish the soil preparation on their own when he went off and left them just when they most needed his encouragement. Tired or no, he should have supervised this part more closely, even if the completion of the job had to be postponed to another day. At the office, he has learned to establish standards and to check on performance with every project his staff undertakes. This is an equally important principle for him to apply at home.

                              *   *   *

No business can operate for long without some kind of planning and the organization necessary to carry out the plan. Nearly all business problems can be attributed to poor planning, lack of organization, or inadequate control of the operation. Critical comments are heard too about the housewife who is a "poor planner" or "completely disorganized." In business there are many guideposts to efficient management, and the modern businessman devotes much time and money to the study of how he can more effectively plan and organize to do a better job. But what help is offered to the long-suffering housewife? No management training course is available to her; no textbook provides a ready answer to all her problems. And yet, like the manager whose balance sheet or income statement leaves something to be desired, she too recognizes the need for help on many occasions. The manager is more fortunate in that he can be transferred to another job to get away from his daily pressures if they become too great, but the lady of the house cannot change jobs. She is committed to make the best of it right where she is. What then can she do to improve matters at home?

Planning is the most important practical part of running home or office. Everything the housewife or the businessman does is part of some kind of plan. A plan is a projected course of action. Proper planning, whether it is determining production figures at the factory or the supper menu at home, requires deciding in advance what shall be done. Mother may occasionally reach for the peanut butter and a loaf of bread as part of her last-resort meal preparation, but even this is one kind of planning. A plan may be formed to fix day-to-day or even hour-to-hour schedules. Or a plan may establish long-range policies or goals, map programs, or determine specific methods and procedures.

The business textbooks talk of various types of plans which can be applied in the office or factory. We think they are equally applicable at home. Just as the salesman has his quota, for example, we should think in terms of certain *goals* for the home. A goal, or universally understood statement of purpose, may be applied to various aspects of running the household. Balancing the budget, or planning one vacation per year away from home, is a worthy goal, even if one seldom seems to attain it.

Another type of plan provides a continuing *guide* to business or home operations. The long-range goal of balancing the budget, mentioned above, requires determining in advance certain methods or policies of savings or bookkeeping which will help us achieve it. This is the type of plan which may be used over and over again, or continuously.

A third type of plan is the *project* which is a distinct unit in itself, either short-term or long-range as the situation may demand. Within the family budget framework, we may establish a special money-raising scheme or a savings plan for Junior's bicycle or summer camp. Such special projects should fit into the over-all family plan.

A plan should be based on a clearly defined objective, and should include standards for its achievement. It should be flexible and simple, and should make use of available resources. Good planning, as opposed to the peanut-butter-sandwich approach, requires time, determined effort, and an unselfish attitude. Father should not close his mind to all interests but his own love of fishing when planning a vacation, and Mother should be as objective as possible when considering what to include in the family budget. Just as a successful business has no room for snap judgments or hasty decisions, similarly emotional hunches or selfish whims have no part in the planning procedures of the well-run home.

Planning requires an analytical approach. Do you have budgetary problems and do they need attention? *"Always"* is the universal reply. But mere recognition of the existence of this ever-pressing household stumbling block is not enough. We must proceed beyond this point in order to isolate and clarify the trouble spots.

Still thinking in terms of the budget as a typical planning venture, the next step is to see what alternatives there are. *More money or go hungry,* we may say. And then we stop and throw up our hands. But if we can overcome this emotional impasse long enough to uncover additional alternatives, we can then assemble the facts and analyze the courses of action suggested by each.

Of course, all family planning is not that simple. A few general statements will not balance your budget or ours. But a more scientific approach to such a plan may keep us from family spats and general misunderstanding. A plan provides a deterrent to irrational action. Once it is agreed on, the family budget may have to be changed occasionally, but at least its very existence helps keep the temptation of the moment from interfering with our long-range objective of making ends meet. It provides some guidance when we see the attractive new spring clothes in the window downtown. Before we rush in to buy a complete Easter outfit, at least we may hesitate long enough to ask ourselves: "Is it in the budget?" or "What can I cut out in order to afford this?"

An over-all plan will prevent minor crises from interfering with the achievement of long-term projects. Mopping up the milk the baby spilled just when you are serving a well-planned meal to your hungry off-spring may delay the meal slightly, but need not throw the whole family into a state of confusion. If we are disorganized and have no general plan or schedule at all, such incidents make matters far worse. We may be unavoidably delayed when we plan to leave for the shore by nine o'clock, or to get the children off to school by eight-thirty sharp, but at least we have something to aim for. By following a regular schedule we will undoubtedly have the youngsters in school on time more often than if we let them drift along on their own. It sometimes seems as though they might never make it at all without some effort on Mother's part.

With some systematized procedure we can keep the job from running us. We are critical of the business-man who does nothing but "put out fires." He is the fellow who never seems able to follow any plan for getting his work done because something is always coming up to interfere. His counterpart in the next office may have comparable problems, but because he has carefully scheduled his own time as well as that of those who work for him, he never seems to be in a rush and he usually meets his deadlines. This may be a matter of personality differences, but it is more likely to be a matter of training, self-discipline, and intelligent planning.

We all know people who seem disorganized all the time. They ask their more efficient friends: "How do you do it, with all those children?" We all have our planning and organizing to do, whether it is merely a

Reg Hider, *Christian Science Monitor*

"Are you sure you wouldn't like peaches?"

list of things to do for the day, which can be written down over coffee after the children have left for school, or something worked out after much family discussion. Organizing is the grouping of necessary activities which will allow you to carry out your plans. It gives structure to the plan and is a guide to carrying it to completion.

The good planner in business rarely runs out of material or tools to do his job. One criterion of the successful housewife is the state of the family larder. No last-minute trips to the store for coffee; no hasty calls to Father at the office to bring home a loaf of bread. At least Father does not get many such calls if Mother is doing an efficient job—he is more likely to have the shopping list in his pocket when he leaves for work.

After Mother has planned the family menus she cannot sit back and assume that the job is done. She has work to do. She must think in terms of what is available, to carry out her plans. Will there be anyone at home to help shell the peas? Will there be enough room in the kitchen for baking if the week's ironing is still spread around? Is there enough flour for a cake, and a large enough kettle for the stew? Is there time for the frozen strawberries to thaw? And where is the recipe for Father's favorite frosting?

This example of the essentials of good domestic organizing may seem oversimplified, but the point is that no matter what you are planning you must think in terms of people to help, work space and facilities, materials, tools or equipment, methods, and—most important—*time*. Without at least fleeting consideration of all these elements a good plan for your Sunday dinner may never come off.

It is not enough merely to consider what is at your disposal to help carry out your plans. It is also important to use these resources efficiently. It is here that we separate the calm of the organized household from the chaotic bedlam of the well-planned but ineptly run home.

Business people spend a lot of time in finding how to make the most of their human resources. A successful business carefully defines each worker's responsibilities and his relationship to the organization, and makes sure that there is no one on the payroll who has nothing to do. At home we may not need an organization chart, but we should be aware of children's capacities, training, and weaknesses as we organize the daily task of running family affairs. Make the best use of the talent available, meager as it may seem when your children are young. Are you babying your youngest child? Can he do more to help? Does he want to? Is six-year-old Danny big enough to put the trash into the incinerator? Now that Sue has her driver's license, can she run some of the errands? Getting things done through others should be part of your planning, as pointed out in Chapter V on delegation. Working together with your children will produce the best results, and afford an opportunity for training and development. In this manner they will also learn to respect and appreciate what it takes to keep the household in good working order.

Unless you are rattling around in a twenty-room mansion you probably feel that your work space is inadequate. Have you surveyed it to see how it can be expanded? Is there room in the kitchen for Father to put up another shelf? Since your own bedroom closet is overcrowded, how about using Junior's for the summer things? He has so few thing—clothes, that is. How much extra walking are you doing because of the arrangement of the kitchen? It is not necessary to be an efficiency engineer to see household short cuts. Just take a careful look around you. What have you done to provide space for the children to do their homework? Does Father have a work-bench area where he can make household repairs easily, or does every job take half an hour longer than necessary because he has to clear a space and round up the tools he needs? We are all too likely to go on doing things the same way for years without stopping to analyze whether it is the best and easiest way. One caution, though, Father—try to be tactful when you show Mother how inefficient she has been not to make better use of all that space under the sink. There is no need to sacrifice domestic harmony for the sake of a few cubic feet of storage space.

In the shop or office, extensive study and training programs insure the best use of tools and equipment. At home we seldom give enough time and study to efficient use of the various household appliances and conveniences we have at hand. There are always some shiny new ones we would like to have, if only the budget would permit. But in the meantime are we using the ones we have properly? How do we store our equipment? Is it convenient? Perhaps it is true that we have insufficient space, as most of us would maintain. If so, that is all the more reason for organizing our equipment properly in what space we have. Are the things we use every day handy, and the once-a-month items on the back of the shelf?

The matter of equipment also comes into a long-term budgeting plan. At home we do not do enough of the thoughtful study that goes into equipment planning in business. The factory manager does not keep an obsolete machine which is now a time-consuming liability or an operating danger. He weighs what each piece of equipment is producing against the output and cost of newer, more modern machinery. Similarly at home, despite the ever-existing family debt, we should sometimes consider purchasing a new washing machine or a new car to save money. There may be all kinds of hazards, expenses, and liabilities involved in continuing to use worn-out equipment, particularly if it is electrical. We do not suggest that because the three-year-old car needs two new tires it would be less expensive to buy the new four-thousand-dollar miracle in the dealer's window; only that it is a good idea to take a close look now and then at the tools you now are using to run the household.

In business most routine operations are carried out according to stated methods and procedures. The armed forces spell out to the last wiggle of the little finger how things are to be done, to the extent that "How to Build a Box" may be the subject of a thirty-six page manual. At home we have available to us books on child care, cooking, gardening, and carpentry, but what guide have we to efficiency in other routine chores? Think about the family washing, for example. If you have a clothes drier, do you still take time to hang out the clothes every sunny day? Do you know whether or not it is really more efficient to dig the dandelions by hand instead of using weedkiller?

All this leads to the most important single item of organization—*time*. To some extent everything we have discussed involves the best use of this essential commodity. There are not enough hours in the day, we all agree. But what are you doing about budgeting the hours you have? If necessary, deadlines should be established, study schedules checked, and Father's weekends organized in advance to allow some time for relaxation as well as work.

The balance between human resources and available physical facilities will need a review now and then. How much is Mother's time worth? Because time saved for her does not mean more production and more money in the bank, as it would in business, we may not feel it necessary to put it into monetary terms. But the well-run house with the well-organized housewife undoubtedly gets a good return on investment in the form of happiness and satisfaction. How much is it worth to save half an hour a day with an automatic washing machine? This does not have to be translated into dollars, but it might be an interesting experiment to figure the cost of a new machine over a period of months and contrast it with time Mother now spends with the family wash. Whether or not you figure it in terms of dollars and cents, never overlook the boost it might give to her morale.

In giving structure to our plans through organizing, there are certain mechanical aids which may help us get things done. Lists of jobs or schedules made out daily or weekly, with priorities allocated for each, may keep us from a frustrated feeling of not knowing what to fly at first. Many times there seems to be so much to do that we sit down helplessly and do nothing. Some of this time could be better spent in analyzing which things should be done first; how long each one will take; and which ones could be completed quickly and easily as a means of balancing the work schedule. What can a good wife do when Father states on Saturday morning that he wants to wash the car, clean out the garage, mow the lawn, paint the bathroom and repair the radio, and that he just does not see how he can get it all done? Lead him gently to his easy chair and start over again. Which of the jobs has he really set his heart on completing by Sunday evening? How about leaving a little time for fun? And what will happen if the Frenches stop by to discuss the next P.T.A. meeting? If there is no room in Father's plan for such interruptions the weekend may be spoiled for the whole family.

It is helpful to establish some kind of a reasonable

schedule for each day, with time allowed for all the necessary jobs—and preferably for eating and sleeping as well. At the end of the day, review it to see how well you did: what has had to be postponed until next week and what can be carried over until tomorrow. By all means cross off what is completed as you go along—the blacker the pencil the better, that is half the satisfaction of keeping a list. You may want to keep a running list as well as a daily one. In either case, be sure to keep it flexible and revise it often.

Other lists and inventories can help bring office efficiency into the home. Part of being well organized is to know exactly what is in the freezer or who has borrowed the latest whodunit, but few of us can keep such facts in mind without some written reminder. Lists of books you or your children would like to read are helpful too. A family reading list will make it possible for you to suggest books to your children when they ask, and may also serve as an aid to scheduling your own reading. You may seldom find time to read anything but the headlines, but at least you will know what to pull off the library shelf if the opportunity does arise. Lists of recurring expenses and a carefully maintained record of major expenses, past or future, will prove useful when you make up your budget as well as when you are tempted to use this week's paycheck on some unbudgeted extra. Any insurance man will advise you to keep lists of household furnishings and costs in the event that you have to prove a loss due to theft or fire or other damage.

You may also want to consider other office methods and equipment to provide a well-organized approach to domestic life. There is no need to turn the living room into an office, but somewhere in the house a real working desk is an essential. In it, or nearby in a file drawer or cabinet, you can keep lists and documents, income tax figures, and all kinds of directions such as how to maintain the power mower or wash the baby's new blanket. Household bookkeeping will be more businesslike if you recognize that a desk or file drawer is the place to keep the books.

Even minor gadgets can add to the efficiency of the home. How many households own a pencil sharpener that really sharpens? Surprisingly few; and yet this can be extremely handy in a location that is convenient to all members of the family—except perhaps those small members who are fond of dumping the shavings out on the floor. Other inexpensive gadgets which are common to the office and make valuable additions to your well-run household include clipboards for current marketing and work lists; bulletin boards; a stapler or two; and plenty of Scotch tape. Rubber name stamps may help; a paper cutter is not to be overlooked when your children are of scrapbook age; and paper clips, rubber bands, and all manner of office trivia will prove useful if you keep them in a central spot, such as the desk.

Once well-laid plans are carefully organized and put into motion, we may feel that at last we can rank as model husband or housewife. But one thing remains as an important part of budget making or vacation scheduling. This is making sure that the results of our efforts conform as nearly as possible to our original plan. We must check, regulate, test and verify our organizing to be certain that as we go along with this budget or schedule we really are keeping within its confines. We must look at the bank balance—if any—at regular intervals, and try to keep all creditors happy while adhering to our economic plan for survival.

In order to exercise control over an established scheme for running the home, we may want to set up some kind of steppingstones which we can reach along the way toward completion of a successful plan. Mother knows enough to check the roast in the oven now and then, and Father makes sure that there is enough gas in the car for the weekend jaunt; but do they also know in advance how they are going to keep the budget in balance, control expenditures, find the time to maintain such an extensive vegetable garden, and really keep track of the family situation in general? Everyone in the family has to realize the part he should play in making a plan for a family project or summer vacation a reality. This goes beyond good organization on the part of one parent. It is necessary to get everyone in the family interested in carrying out the plan. This may mean looking into the actions of other members of the family, checking their performance, and comparing their results with what has been planned. Whenever necessary, one parent may have to put a firm foot down, as would be the case if Father were tempted to buy a new tweeter for his hi-fi set just when the down payment is due on the summer cottage.

In administering the well-run household, we see that all our recommended techniques of listening to others, conferring with the family, delegating, and communicating with understanding may come to nought if at the same time we do not have in operation some sensible and workable day-to-day and long-range plans. We may work hard to have a beautiful home in which everything is always tidy and a piping-hot dinner served on time each night. But what good is this if we cannot stay within the budget, or if we go to pieces at the thought of trying to give up one afternoon a week to work at the Red Cross? What kind of well-rounded existence is this? Time is the essence of all good planning, and the successful housewife should have not only an orderly home but also time for outside activity and some recreation and reading as well. To accomplish this she must work together with all the family to apply effective methods of planning and organizing to her home.

IX

Family Development:
Guiding, Coaching, and Advising

LET US NOW TAKE a look at what happened at our house recently. The scene opens with Father returning home hot and tired, after battling the Friday evening traffic. Just about everything that could go wrong at the office had done so this day. His usually even-tempered boss had failed to exercise his best managerial techniques, and so on down the line. As Father enters, he catches sight of his children sprawled around the living room reading comic books.

"I thought we had decided you kids weren't going to waste your time reading those junky comics."

No reply.

"Haven't we bought you enough good books? Seems as though we've talked ourselves blue in the face, trying to get some decent reading habits started around here."

"Yeah, Dad."

"Hi, Dad."

"Hello, Pop."

"Well then, let's do something about it. Come on, now. Up on your feet. Let's get rid of that trash. Why aren't you helping your mother? And how about homework? Get moving!"

Mother enters. "Hello, dear."

"Do you see what the children are reading? Why can't you keep this trash out of the house?"

"But Henry, I told them they could read until supper. Besides . . ."

Father's voice grows louder. "I'll bet their homework isn't even started. And look at Jimmy! Why does he have to sprawl all over the new slipcovers? We paid enough for them without having muddy feet all over the place."

"But, dear—" Mother takes the plunge. She has been enjoying a few quiet moments in kitchen, preparing supper without interruption. "I told the children they could read them. They passed them out in school today. And just stop and look a minute—Jimmy's wearing his slippers. Come on now, you need some supper."

Father sputters and grumbles, but is finally persuaded to sit down and read the paper until supper is ready. The children have wisely disappeared, comics in hand.

With supper comes the more friendly atmosphere which Mother had counted on food to provide. After second helpings all round, Father reopens the conversation. "I guess I was sort of mean to you kids before supper. What are those comics, anyway? Mother says you got them at school."

"All about rockets and scientists and stuff."

"I'm supposed to write a report on them—it's part of our homework."

"Gee, yes, they're neat."

Father grimaces. "Guess I was way off base. I'm sorry, boys, I'm so anxious to have you read the right kind of books and magazines that I just blew my stack when I saw the comics. Guess I was hungry."

"They really are good comics, Dad. Maybe you'd like to look them over."

"And we really weren't going to read them all night —I still have some math."

Dessert is served, and peace descends. Are there conclusions to be drawn? They are all very simple:

1. *The boys* figured that Dad came home in a grouchy mood, all right, but knew he'd get over it. Mostly he's a pretty good guy around the house. He just didn't understand about those comics.

2. *Mother* had learned from experience that food would help.

3. *Father* himself was willing to admit that he had been hasty and that he had taken his own bad mood out on the boys. He cares so much about their reading and study habits that sometimes it is difficult not to put on too much pressure. Essentially, though, he admits that they're good kids, and that they have done pretty well this year on buckling down to homework.

4. *Our own conclusion* is that it is not possible for even the most well-ordered household to be one hundred per cent efficient at all times, even in the field of human relations. If Father or Mother goes off the deep end once in a while in a burst of bad management, this should not cancel out the benefits of all their previous attempts to maintain a harmonious household. The main thing is to keep right on trying.

In business or in the home, the development of people is accomplished through a combination of various forms of supervision. These may include counseling and guidance, encouragement through praise and proper motivation, coaching, and appraisal and evaluation after a job is done. Supervising is more than getting work done through others. It goes beyond the good planning and organizing necessary to effective management. It is an active process, not effective in the hands of the manager who leans back in his chair and lets his people run his office or his household. Even in business, supervision cannot be measured wholly in terms of financial success. The good supervisor is aware of his people and their progress as much as he is of the requirements for him to produce a certain amount of work.

The general aims of counseling and guidance are to try to help a person to see his strengths and weaknesses, and to figure out for himself how he can improve. This entails more than the mere giving of advice. When our children ask for help on questions of saving money or getting better marks, we are quick to offer advice. But do we also give them the opportunity to work out the answers for themselves? When we have finished talking to them, have we left them with a firm resolve to save regularly, or to get on the honor roll? A discussion of such questions is of little lasting value to a child if we fail to be specific and pinpoint the problem. In doing so, we should try to avoid interference from side issues and personalities. Jerry's marks are not to be blamed entirely on "that awful teacher" or on his recent case of measles. What about his recent accomplishments or lack of same? Try to base the discussion on facts and matters of record. Look over his school papers and the last report card; have him recall the recent times when television interfered with homework. Do not dwell too long on poor past performance, but use such references to start him thinking about how he can improve.

To be effective, counseling must be positive. We should express as often as possible our confidence in our children and their ability to progress. The constant threat of: "You'll never get this right" or "How do you expect to learn it that way?" will not produce results. Let the child tell you what is wrong; get him to rate himself if possible; then try to agree together on a course of action. It is particularly important that such discussions be constructive and that their results be mutually agreed upon. The more the child can be drawn out to contribute his ideas and suggestions the better. In fact, the degree of success which comes from this type of supervision will be directly related—in an inverse ratio—to the amount of talking, scolding and dictating you do. The techniques discussed in Chapter III on correcting other people apply here, too. Emphasis on the future instead of the past, the reassurance of help, and a plan for a follow-up are all part of your job as the family supervisor.

Problems of motivation and morale are often discussed in business. How do you make people want to work, and enjoy it when they do? How do you get groups to work happily together? These are questions the business manager must face. Sooner or later he will realize that unhappy or resentful workers are not going to produce as well as those whose morale is high, even though the results may be adequate to keep the business running.

At home we may overlook the fact that children too will do better at school and around the house if they have the proper stimulation. When the atmosphere of the home is one of understanding and co-operation, they will respond more willingly both to emergencies and to everyday demands. People of all ages need appreciation and praise, as well as an assurance of support from above. In the parent-child relationship even more than in business it is important to assure a child that we have faith in his abilities, his judgment, and his future. This may be difficult when Bill has just started a fire in the neighbor's garage, or Susan has stolen a dime from the piggy bank of the little boy upstairs. But try we must, and even in these difficult situations our criticism should be tactful, constructive, and above all private. It is important for the child's morale that he be assured of support even when he is at fault.

Encouragement is a necessary part of supervisory responsibility. Industry has found it essential to take an interest in its workers and to let them know how important each one is to the company. At home too, parents should recognize the need for individual and group discussion of school work, home projects, outside sports and social activities. Personal consideration and encouragement for each child are vital. The result may be disastrous if you pass out all the bouquets to Johnny for his good report card, but have nothing good at all to say to his sister. Surely you can think of *something* to say to her, if only to assure her that she "belongs," that despite reverses she is an important part of the family. With proper encouragement even the lowliest sweeper in the factory develops pride in his work and his contribution to the business, and feels up until the day he retires that "they really can't do without me." Your children should have the same feeling at home: that they belong, that they occupy an important position in the family—not that they are always underfoot, or that you would prefer them to be "seen and not heard" according to the outworn adage.

Praise is a big factor in bolstering morale and counteracting fear of failure. Even when morale is high and encouragement frequent, a dash of praise is the final touch, the extra ingredient which brings out the full flavor of the developmental stew. Parents should compliment whenever possible. They should try to find something to praise in even the youngest child or the poorest worker, no matter how hard they have to search to find it. We do not mean to advocate constant flattery or hollow praise, just that you look for the good rather than the bad or the incomplete, and give credit when and where it is due.

All the encouragement and commendation in the world will not produce results if we fail to set a good example by actually working at a job ourselves instead of directing it from the comfort of our favorite armchair. Industry has found that classroom discussion and textbook training can only supplement on-the-job supervision or coaching. This does not mean that the shop foreman runs through the whole operation for each new man and then leaves him to be on his own. Good coaching allows plenty of opportunity for the worker to perform, with the foreman in the role of guide and coach. Parents should give some thought to how they bring their children along in sports, games and household skills. Father cannot teach the boys how to kick a football from the living room. On the other hand, if when he steps outside he proceeds to do all the kicking himself, he is not going to be very successful either. He must give the boys the opportunity to perform themselves, and try not to grab the ball away to demonstrate every time they get off a poor kick.

Coaching can be either a team or an individual effort. The main thing is that an atmosphere of mutual confidence and respect should be established. Certainly, Father, the boys know you can kick the ball better and farther than they. But how do they feel about your willingness and ability to pass on your knowledge to them? What kind of a goal are you giving them to shoot for if you get off your best punt since leaving Central High and tell them simply that *this* is the way to do it? It is discouraging for your seven- and nine-year-old boys to be faced with having to duplicate your best efforts, whether they are in football, checkers, or a carpentry project. Part of the coaching responsibility is to set up reasonable standards for the young people and help them to progress toward them.

At school the children are given a periodic appraisal of their school work through report cards. Perhaps you should think in terms of similar evaluations at home once in a while. In this way you can do more than just praise and encourage. You can offer guidance through constructive interest in the work of the children. It may be impossible to grade your children on everything they do, but occasionally you might want to take an objective look at Ralph's lawn mowing and discuss it in terms of his and your expectations. Appraising people in accordance with their performance is a continuing process. All of us, consciously or unconsciously, apply our standards to practically everything done by those with whom we come in contact. So why not make it official every now and then, by grading Ralph in Sixth-grade Lawn Mowing, and talking to him about it?

One approach to this rating of work performance which has been tried successfully in business is to let people evaluate their own accomplishments as a means of introducing a constructive discussion on the job. Perhaps by letting Ralph tell us how he thinks the lawn mowing is going, we may find it easier to make any necessary corrections and improvements. Such a discussion should take place while the job is being done or immediately after it is completed. How does Ralph think the lawn compares with others in the neighborhood? What can be improved? Let him know how you feel and what praise or criticism may have been heard from others. Letting him know how other people view his work will make him more interested in trying to improve. If you merely find fault, with comments of "you missed a place" or "why didn't you trim the edges?," the discussion will not be particularly helpful to him—and you may find that you have to do it yourself the next time, just as you did before he was big enough to push the mower.

Up to this point we have been discussing some specific elements of good supervision, just as in earlier chapters we talked about specific techniques of business management that may be used at home. Now we want to discuss home management from a different point of view, in an attempt to point out that the application of these various techniques should be a part of the development of all members of the family, including the parents themselves. In its broader sense, this development is the process of establishing short and long-range goals for helping the family to grow, and of striving to reach them by means of a favorable attitude toward such growth and the creation of an atmosphere in which it can take place.

In running a family, we have to think not only of getting the task at hand completed pleasantly and effectively, but also of what our work assignments and projects are doing to make us better people. Is Father easier to live with now that he has worked out a better scheme for cleaning out the garage or planning the family outing? Does Mother get more satisfaction from preparing meals now that she finds it is not a case of shooing her children out of the kitchen, but of getting their helpful support? And are the children doing less squabbling now that they have learned to bring their chief differences of opinion to be mediated at the weekly family conference?

These are examples of the goals involved in our program of using at home some of the human relations techniques which business has found useful. We should also look beyond such immediate objectives toward the future. The effectiveness of the day-to-day supervision of our children must be measured in terms of their future development: the type of adults they will become; the successes or failures they may have as they grow up. Our efforts are confined to helping, guiding, and pointing the way. We cannot develop our children—this they must do themselves.

Our attitude toward our children, toward their schools, their activities and everything in their lives is going to affect them more than any direct supervision. Human relations skills carefully applied, and all the

Doris Matthews, *Christian Science Monitor*

"Now they are saying that if you teach them to integrate with the group, they lose their individuality."

lessons that we can learn from business, are mere supplements to the day-to-day home scene as it influences the children. A sporadic effort to be better parents or an occasional reference to a book for a solution to a specific problem will not go nearly as far as a continuing effort to create the right atmosphere in the home. We hope that this book will help, but it cannot be expected to correct impressions left on children who grow up with feuding parents, profane or abusive fathers, or whining, complaining mothers.

A vital part of the atmosphere of the home is provided by the example set by the parents in their attitude toward the world outside the home and toward their own continued growth and development. Business emphasizes that all development is self-development. Certainly if an aspiring young man does not wish to help himself to grow, all the textbooks and fancy training courses will teach him nothing. Whether we are concerned with the businessman or the housewife, we see that it is the person who has a lively interest in his job, the community, and life in general who is contributing the most to his own self-development. Such a person has acquired a habit of never being satisfied that the best possible job is being done. He manages to keep abreast of new thoughts and ideas, and is willing to take a chance on the new and untried.

People with inquiring minds may be criticized as odd in that they do not always conform to established or accepted standards. The housewife who is interested in self-improvement may get carried away by her role of "do-gooder." She may become so active in community affairs that her motives are misconstrued. She may overdo it, or be misdirected onto some peculiar tangent. At the same time she is undoubtedly getting more out of life than her friend down the road who spends her waking moments keeping the living room spotless, and letting off steam through compulsive scrubbing and polishing. They may both use up the same amount of energy, but our community-minded friend brings home a mental stimulation and an enthusiastic interest in the outside world; whereas her homebound friend is probably too tired at night to read more than the front page of the local newspaper, and may leave to her husband the whole tiresome business of keeping informed. The role of the thinking parent is to take part, to go beyond the mechanics of homemaking in order to make a worth-while contribution to the growth of both family and community.

Budgeting of time is one of the main problems of self-development. We have talked about the businessman who never has time for anything extra because of the pressures of the job at hand, and who is baffled by the success of his well-organized counterpart. At home it takes both organization and self-discipline, plus occasional neglect of the pots and pans in the sink or the weeds in the garden, to make time to read beyond the headlines; to study the recommendations of the local authorities for changes in the schools; to investigate the pros and cons of legislation at state or national levels. It is not enough to have a few more facts than the people next door, or to gather a smattering of knowledge to impress your friends at the church social. Being well informed and willing to consider all sides of a question is a source of greater satisfaction than the knowledge that the beds are always made by eight o'clock (A.M.) or that the children are always perfectly groomed.

There is so much concern in business with the volume of reading required that many companies have inaugurated courses to increase the reading speed of their employees. At home we may think that we have only enough time to read part of the daily papers, but once again it is to be emphasized that with planning and organization we can create the time for more reading. Then we can make a broader selection of worth-while books and periodicals which will help us keep up with the world outside and at the same time provide pleasure and relaxation.

The mental alertness of parents who are interested in self-development is bound to be reflected in the attitudes of their children as they grow. However, it is not enough to hope that some of your personality traits will rub off on Junior, or be inherited by Sister. Progressive business organizations long ago abandoned the notion that executives are born, not made. It takes conscious effort on the part of supervisors, either at the office or in the home, to develop people and prepare them for the future.

Parents have a tendency to leave too much of this developmental responsibility to the schools. When a child does not seem to be capable of making his own decisions or thinking intelligently about his school work or other activities, they may harangue the teachers, or hastily transfer him to a private school which has been recommended for its ability to teach young people to make decisions and to develop good study habits. We feel that this training is more appropriately carried on at home. It is the job of the parents to instill proper habits and attitudes, not the duty of the teachers, who must cram a lot of subject matter into five or six hours a day.

Children must be allowed to express their own ideas and to participate in family planning and decision making. At the same time they need some direction, and must learn to respect authority. It is up to the parents to make sure that their direction is helpful without being too restrictive. The budding young man in business who is given no room for expression of his ideas, or time for independent thinking, will soon lose his enthusiasm, or quit and go elsewhere. Business knows that these failures are costly and may strip the organization of its best potential talent. A forward-looking management will try to strike a balance beween individual freedom and authority. In the same manner, parents must make a continuing effort to give their children the challenge of freedom, to guide them to think without trying to guide their thinking.

Parents must provide direction. They must use insight and intelligence in determining the right course of action for themselves and their children. They must be aware of changes in each individual child, and be able to assess readiness for growth at every level. Only in this way can they apply the understanding and guidance which will provide the right kind of development for the child and the most satisfaction for themselves. A large responsibility? An enormous reward.

SUGGESTED ADDITIONAL READING

MAGAZINES

Advanced Management, The Society for the Advancement of Management, Inc., 74 Fifth Avenue, New York, N.Y.

Business Horizons, Indiana University School of Business, Bloomington, Indiana

Dun's Review and Modern Industry, Dun and Bradstreet Publications Corp., New York, N.Y.

Factory Management and Maintenance, McGraw Hill, New York, N.Y.

Harvard Business Review, Graduate School of Business Administration, Harvard University, Cambridge, Mass.

Management Methods Magazine, Management Magazines, Inc., Greenwich, Conn.

Nation's Business, Chamber of Commerce of the United States, Washington, D.C.

Personnel, American Management Association, Inc., 1515 Broadway, New York, N.Y.

Personnel Journal, Personnel Journal, Inc., Swarthmore, Penna.

The Journal of Communication, The National Society for the Study of Communication, Albany, N.Y.

The Management Review, The American Management Association, Inc., 1515 Broadway, New York, N.Y.

BOOKS

Allen, Louis A., *Management and Organization*. McGraw Hill, New York, N.Y., 1958.

Argyris, Chris, *Personality and Organization*. Harper and Bros., New York, N.Y., 1957.

Bursk, Edward C., ed., *Human Relations for Management*. Harper and Bros., New York, N.Y., 1950–56.

Chase, Stuart, *Power of Words*. Harcourt Brace and Co., New York, N.Y., 1954.

Clark, Charles, H., *Brainstorming*. Doubleday and Co., New York, N.Y., 1958.

Drucker, Peter F., *The Practice of Management*. Harper and Bros., New York, N.Y., 1957.

Effective Communication on the Job, The American Management Association, New York, N.Y., 1956.

Hayakawa, S. I., *Language, Meaning, and Maturity*. Harper and Bros., New York, N.Y., 1954.

Josephs, Ray, *Streamlining Your Executive Workload*. Prentice Hall, New York, N.Y., 1958.

Keyes, Kenneth S., Jr., *How to Develop Your Thinking Ability*. McGraw Hill, New York, N.Y., 1950.

Laird, Donald A. and Eleanor C., *Delegating; How to Get Things Done Through Others*. McGraw Hill, New York, N.Y., 1957.

Leavitt, Harold J., *Managerial Psychology*. University of Chicago Press, Chicago, Ill., 1958.

Lee, Irving J., *How to Talk With People*. Harper and Bros., New York, N.Y., 1952.

Lee, Irving J. and Laura L., *Handling Barriers in Communications*. Harper and Bros., New York, N.Y., 1956, 1957.

Murphy, Dennis, *Better Business Communication*. McGraw Hill, New York, N.Y., 1957.

Phillips, David C., *Oral Communication in Business*. Mc-Graw Hill, New York, N.Y., 1955.

Steckle, Lynde C., *The Man in Management*. Harper and Bros., New York, N.Y., 1958.

Thelen, Herbert A., *Dynamics of Groups at Work*. University of Chicago Press, Chicago, Ill., 1954.

Urwick, Lyndall, *The Elements of Administration*. Harper and Bros., New York, N.Y., 1943.

Index